PRACTICAL and
PERPLEXING
QUESTIONS
ANSWERED

PRACTICAL and PERPLEXING QUESTIONS ANSWERED

by

R. A. TORREY

MOODY PRESS
CHICAGO

PRACTICAL and PERPLEXING
QUESTIONS ANSWERED

ANGELS

Please explain Matthew 18:10: "Take heed that ye despise not one of these little ones; for I say unto you, that in heaven their angels do always behold the face of my Father which is in heaven." Has every child a guardian angel?

This seems to be the plain teaching of the text. Some explain the text in another way, that the angels of the children spoken of here are the departed spirits of the children in the glory, but there is not a hint in the Bible anywhere that the departed spirits of human beings are angels. The clearest distinction is kept all through the Bible between angels and men. The old hymn "I Want to Be an Angel" has no warrant whatever in Scripture.

The angels of the children here spoken of are the angels who watch over the children. It is the office of angels to minister in behalf of those who shall be heirs of salvation (Hebrews 1:14), and each child seems, according to the Bible, to have a guardian angel, and these angels occupy a position of special favor and opportunity before God. They stand in His very presence and always behold the face of the Father.

ANNIHILATION OF THE WICKED

What is meant by the theory of the annihilation of the wicked? Is it scriptural?

It means the annihilation of being of those who die without having accepted Jesus Christ as their Saviour.

There is no Scripture to support such a theory. The Bible clearly teaches that the future destiny of the wicked is a

5

condition of unresting, unending, conscious torment and anguish. See further answer under "Eternal Punishment."

Why is the theory of the annihilation of the wicked, apparently indicated by Revelation 20:14, 15, a reprehensible doctrine, apart from scriptural teaching relating thereto?

The annihilation of the wicked is not indicated in Revelation 20:14, 15 to any one who reads the whole passage and parallel passages in the Scriptures: "And death and hell were cast into the lake of fire. This is the second death. And whosoever was not found written in the book of life was cast into the lake of fire." The lot of those cast into the lake of fire is not annihilation.

As to its being "a reprehensible doctrine, apart from Scripture," I would say that I have never known anyone to accept this doctrine who did not lose power for God. I could tell of instances of men whom God greatly used who have been led to accept this doctrine and who in consequence were in part or altogether set aside as soul-winners. If one really believes the doctrine of the endless, conscious torment of the impenitent he will work as never before for their salvation before it is too late.

ANTICHRIST

Who is the Antichrist, and when will he appear?

The Antichrist will be a person in whom Satan's resistance to Christ and His kingdom will culminate. He will be a man, but a man whom Satan will fill to such an extent that he will be Satan incarnate. The Devil always seeks to ape God's work, and his aping of God's work will culminate in his aping of the incarnation of God in Jesus Christ. The Antichrist's coming will be after the working of Satan, with all power and signs and wonders of falsehood, and with all deceit of unrighteousness (II Thessalonians 2:9, 10, R. V., margin).

He will appear just previous to the coming of Jesus Christ, and our Lord will consume him with the breath of His mouth

6

and destroy him with the brightness of His coming (II Thessalonians 2:8, R. V.).

There are already many antichrists preparing the way for the final and consummate Antichrist (I John 2:18). Indeed, every one that denieth the Father and the Son is an antichrist, but there seems to be an especial preparation for *the* Antichrist, in whom all the forces of evil shall head up, in the papacy on the one hand and in rationalism and anarchy on the other hand. The papacy, the anarchistic socialism and rationalism some day will join and be headed by one man whom the Devil shall especially gift and in whom he shall dwell, and that man will be the Antichrist.

ASSURANCE OF SALVATION

Is it right for a person to say that he is saved before he dies?

May I know that I am saved, and if so, on what authority?

If you really are saved you may know it on the authority of God's Word. God says in John 3:36: "He that believeth on the Son *hath* everlasting life." You know whether you believe on the Son or not. If you do believe on the Son you know you have everlasting life because God here says so in so many words.

Again, I John 5:11, 12: "This is the record, that God hath given to us eternal life, and this life is in His Son. He that hath the Son *hath* life, and he that *hath not* the Son of God, *hath not* life." For one who believes on the Son to doubt he has life is to make God a liar. We are told this in so many words in the preceding verse, where we read: "He that believeth not God hath made Him a liar, because he believeth not the record that God gave of His Son."

Furthermore, anyone who has received Jesus as his Saviour and Lord and King may know that he is a child of God. God says so in so many words in John 1:12: "But as many as received Him to them gave He power to become the sons of God." If you have received Jesus you have a right to call yourself a child of God. You have no right to doubt that you are a child of God.

Again, every one that believes on Jesus has a right to know that he is justified, that his sins are all forgiven, and that God counts him righteous in Christ. He has a right to know it on the very best ground, namely, because God says so. We read in Acts 13:38, 39: "Be it known unto you therefore, men and brethren, that through this Man is preached unto you forgiveness of sins, and by Him *all that believe are justified* from all things." Notice, it says: "All that believe are justified." You know whether you believe or not. If you do believe on Jesus, God says you are justified. Many people doubt their salvation because they look at their feelings instead of looking at the Word of God. It is not a question at all whether you *feel* that you are a child of God, it is simply a question of what God says, and if you look at your feelings instead of the Word of God you make God a liar for the sake of your own feelings.

God caused one book of the Bible to be written for the very purpose that every one that believes on the Son of God *might know* that he has eternal life (I John 5:13): "These things (are) written unto you that believe on the name of the Son of God, *that ye may know* that ye have eternal life." If God caused a book to be written that we might know it, then certainly we may know it, and the verse teaches us that the way to know it is from what is "written." The first thing to be sure of is that you really do believe on Jesus, that you really have received Him as your Saviour, surrendered to Him as your Lord and Master, confessed Him as such publicly before the world. When sure of that you may be absolutely sure that you are saved, that you have eternal life, that your sins are all forgiven, that you are a child of God.

THE ATONEMENT

What theory of the atonement does the Bible teach?

The Bible does not teach a *theory* of atonement—it teaches *a fact,* the glorious fact that every one of our sins was laid upon Jesus Christ (Isaiah 53:6; I Peter 2:24; II Corinthians 5:21; Galatians 3:13), and that through Jesus Christ having borne our sins there is not only pardon for every sin but justification, which is more than pardon. That is, the Bible teaches that as Jesus Christ took our place on the cross, the moment we accept Jesus Christ we step into His place, the place of perfect acceptance before God, we become the righteousness of God in Him (II Corinthians 5:12, R. V.). We no longer have our own poor, pitiable, unsatisfactory righteousness, but a perfect righteousness, the righteousness of God in Christ (Philippians 3:9, R. V.).

How could God punish His innocent Son for the guilt of man?

The doctrine of the Bible is not that God, a holy first person, takes the sins of man, a guilty second person, and lays them upon His own holy Son, an innocent third person. That is the way the doctrine is often misrepresented. In fact, it is the representation usually made by those who reject the Bible doctrine of substitution.

The real teaching of the Bible is that Jesus Christ is not a third person, that He is indeed the first person, "that God was in Christ reconciling the world unto himself" (II Corinthians 5:19), and that in the atoning death of His Son, instead of laying the punishment of guilty man upon an innocent third person, God took the shame and suffering due to man upon Himself; and so far from that being unjust and cruel it is amazing grace!

Furthermore, Jesus Christ was the second person. He was not merely *a* man, He was *"the Son of man,"* the representative Man, the head of the race. No ordinary man could bear the guilt of other men, but "the Son of man," the representative Man, could.

If we take the teaching of the Bible not in a fragmentary way but as a complete whole it is the most wonderful philosophy the world has ever known. We will ponder and admire its inexhaustible depths throughout eternity. But if we take any one doctrine out, the other doctrines become absurd. If

9

we give up the doctrine of the deity of Jesus Christ, then the doctrine of the atonement becomes an absurdity, and the difficulty suggested by this question naturally arises. Or if we give up the doctrine of the real humanity of Christ, the doctrine of the atonement loses its profound significance. But if we take all the Bible says, namely, that Jesus was really divine, "God manifest in the flesh" (I Timothy 3:16), and that He was truly man, not merely a man but "the Son of man," the representative Man, then the doctrine of the atonement presents no difficulties but an amazing depth of truth.

It is strange how little the average objector to the doctrine of substitution knows about the real doctrine of the Bible on this point. Instead of fighting what the Bible really teaches he is fiighting a figment of his own uninstructed imagination.

BACKSLIDING

How would you deal with a backslider? Is there hope for him, and how?

Everywhere I go I find many persons who tell me that they were once Christians, but confess that they have gone back into the world. I am persuaded that many of these were never truly saved. They have gone forward in revival meetings, or united with the church, or done something of that sort, but they have never really fully accepted Jesus Christ as Saviour and Lord. Having made a failure of their first attempt, they hesitate to make another.

This hesitation is unreasonable. The fact that one has attempted to do a thing and done it in the wrong way is no reason for not doing it in the right way. If people would begin the Christian life right they would not be so likely to go back, and if they have begun it wrong they had better begin it over again in the better way.

The right way to begin, as shown us by God's own Word, is:

First, to accept Jesus Christ as Saviour that is to believe God's testimony concerning Him, that He bore all your sins

10

in His own body on the cross; and to trust God to forgive you, not because of anything that you have done but because of what Christ did when He made full atonement for your sins in His own body on the cross (I Peter 2:24; Galatians 3:13).

Second, to accept Jesus Christ as your Lord and King (Acts 2:36). This involves the utter surrender of your thoughts to Him to teach, and of your life to Him to govern. You must put yourself completely at His disposal. You must not only sing with your lips but make it a fact in your life—"I surrender all." This lack of absolute surrender at the time of starting the Christian life is the cause of a large measure of backsliding.

Third, to accept Christ as the risen Son of God who has all power in heaven and on earth, and to trust Him to keep you day by day from falling, and from all the power of sin and temptation (Matthew 28:18; Hebrews 7:25; Jude 24).

Having begun right most of the battle is won, but you must go right on in obedience to Christ. Continuance in the Christian life is not at all a question of your strength, but of Christ's.

If you have begun the Christian life once and failed, begin it again and succeed. Many of the strongest Christians today are those who were once backsliders. The apostle Peter himself was once a backslider, but after Pentecost he was one of the mightiest servants of Christ that the world ever saw. Pentecost is possible for you.

No one can be more miserable than the backslider. Jeremiah was certainly right when he said to backsliding Israel: "It is an evil thing and a bitter that thou hast forsaken the Lord thy God." The one who forsakes Christ forsakes the fountain of living waters, and hews himself out cisterns, broken cisterns, that hold no water (Jeremiah 2:13). Let him leave the broken cisterns of the world and come back to Christ, the Fountain of living water.

BAPTISM

Is baptism necessary for salvation?

It depends upon what you mean by "salvation" and by "baptism." Certainly some have found forgiveness of sins and have entered into eternal life without water baptism, as (for example) the thief on the cross (Luke 23:43). There is a large body of believers who do not practice water baptism at all, namely the Friends (or Quakers), and many of the Friends have the consciousness of having their sins forgiven, and God has set His seal upon their acceptance by giving them the gift of the Holy Ghost.

But "salvation" is used in Scripture not merely of forgiveness of sins and eternal life but in a larger sense of all the fullness of blessing that is to be found in Christ. Certainly one cannot enter into all the fullness of blessing that there is in Christ without absolute obedience to Him (Acts 5:32). If there is any commandment of Christ which we know that we do not obey we certainly cannot enjoy fullness of fellowship with Him. Jesus Christ commanded water baptism (Matthew 28:19, 20). He also commanded it through His disciples (Acts 2:38). But there are earnest followers of Christ who do not see in such passages as these a command to baptize or be baptized with water, and in not being baptized they are not consciously disobeying Jesus Christ.

As an act of obedience to Christ, therefore, water baptism certainly is in the larger sense a saving ordinance for those who believe that Jesus Christ commands it. Submitting to baptism has been the turning point in the experience of many a man and many a woman. It has been done as an act of conscious obedience to Jesus Christ, and has been accompanied by great blessing.

It is difficult for me to see how anyone can study the New Testament with the single-eyed purpose of discovering what it actually teaches and not see the necessity of water baptism, and yet from my contact with those believers known as Friends I cannot but believe that many of them are perfectly conscientious in not being baptized with water, and are true children of God.

What is the explanation of I Corinthians 15:29: "What shall they do which are baptized for the dead"?

There seems to have been in Paul's time a custom of those who were alive being baptized in behalf of those who for one reason or another had died without baptism. This is the only reference in Scripture to this custom.

It evidently was not a custom that the Bible commanded or sanctioned. Paul does not sanction it here. He simply refers to it as existing and refers to those that practice it as showing that they believed in the resurrection, for otherwise this baptism for the dead would have no significance. The Mormon church practices the custom today, and this verse which they use as a warrant for it does not support the custom. Many customs crept into the church very early which were not of God, which the apostles did not endorse, and which ought not to be followed by us. Certainly if Paul had wished us to follow this custom he would have said something more about it than he does here. He would at least have endorsed it in this place, and he does not. When we look at the verse carefully we see that Paul not only does not endorse it but by implication rejects it, for he separates himself from the custom by saying: "What shall *they* do which are baptized for the dead?" By this word "they" he not only separates himself from it but separates those to whom he writes from this third party who are baptized for the dead.

This usage was afterwards extended, but only among heretics. It was repudiated by the church.

THE BIBLE

Do you believe in the verbal inspiration of the Bible?

I do. That is, I believe that the writers of the various books in the Bible were guided by the Holy Spirit, not only in the thought to which they gave expression but also in the choice of the words in which they expressed the thought. They

13

"spoke from God, being moved by the Holy Ghost" (II Peter 1:21, R. V.). It was the Holy Ghost who spoke (Hebrews 3:7; 10:15, 16; Acts 28:25). The word uttered was His word (II Samuel 23:2, R. V.). The very words used were the words which the Holy Ghost teaches (I Corinthians 2:13). Nothing could be plainer than Paul's statement: *"In words* which the Spirit teacheth."

The Holy Spirit Himself anticipated all these modern ingenious but unbiblical and false theories regarding His own work in the apostles. The more carefully and minutely one studies the wording of the statements made in the Bible, the more he will become convinced of the marvelous accuracy of the words used to produce the thought. To a superficial student the doctrine of verbal inspiration may appear questionable or even absurd, but any regenerated and Spirit-taught man who ponders the words of Scripture day after day and year after year will become increasingly convinced that the wisdom of God is in the very words used as well as in the thought which is expressed in the words.

It is a very suggestive fact that our difficulties with the Bible rapidly disappear when we come to notice the precise language used. The change of a word or a letter, of a tense, case or number, oftentimes lands a person in contradiction or untruth; but by taking the words just as written, difficulties disappear and the truth shines forth. The more microscopically we study the Bible, the more clearly does its divine origin shine forth as we see its perfection of form as well as substance.

Are all parts of the Bible equally inspired by God?

All Scripture is given by inspiration of God, that is, is God-breathed (II Timothy 3:16). There is no warrant for the change that the Revised Version makes in this passage. As originally written the entire Bible was infallible truth, and in our English version we have the original writings given with substantial accuracy.

But not all parts of the Bible are equally *important*. For

14

example, the genealogies given in I Chronicles 1 to 9 are important, far more important than the average student of the Bible realizes, but they certainly are not as important to the believer today as the teachings of Christ and the apostles.

If the Holy Spirit is the author of the words of Scripture, how do we account for variations in style and diction? That, for example, Paul always uses Pauline language and John Johannean language, and so on?

Even if we could not account at all for this fact, it would have little weight against the explicit statements of God's Word. Any one who is humble enough and wise enough to recognize that there are a great many things which we cannot account for at all which could be easily accounted for if we knew a little more, is never staggered by an apparent difficulty of this kind. But in point of fact it is easy enough to account for these variations. The simple explanation is this: the Holy Spirit is wise enough and has facility enough in the use of language in revealing truth to and through any individual to use words, phrases and forms of expression which are in that person's vocabulary and forms of thought to which that person is accustomed, and in every way to make use of that person's peculiar individuality. It is one of the many marks of the divine wisdom of this book that the same divine truth is expressed with absolute accuracy in such widely varying forms of expression.

If the Bible is verbally inspired, why do not the Gospel writers give Jesus' and other persons' words exactly? I can understand how their accounts of acts may differ, but His words cannot properly be rendered one way by Matthew and another way by Luke if verbal inspiration, as applied for instance to Galatians 3:16 ("seeds" or "seed"), is correct.

The Gospel writers do give "person's words" exactly when it claims to give them exactly. When they only claim to give the substance of what they said they may not be given exactly. But while they give Jesus' words exactly they do not always claim to give all that He said, so Matthew may give part of what He said, and Luke another part of what He said, and to get all that He said both accounts must be taken. Matthew gives the part that was adapted to his purpose, and Luke the part that was adapted to his. It is well that they are given in just this way, for it is one of the many incidental proofs that the Gospels are independent of one another and not composed in collusion with one another.

Furthermore, it must be borne in mind that the words of Jesus given by Matthew and Luke were spoken in Aramaic and translated by Matthew and Luke into Greek. There is reason to suppose that the utterances recorded by Matthew, Mark and Luke were largely utterances that Jesus gave in Aramaic, while those recorded by John were largely those that Jesus spoke in Greek, for it must be remembered that in the time of Jesus the people in Palestine were a bilingual people.

Can I depend on the dates given in the margin of the Bible?

No, not at all. The dates in the margin of the Bible are not a part of the original text. They are the result of Archbishop Ussher's work, very good for one of his time, and in a general way give an idea of when things occurred; but great advances have been made in Biblical scholarship since his day, and we now know that some of his dates are utterly unreliable.

How would you endeavor to interest an indifferent person in the study of the Bible?

First of all, I should get him to accept Jesus Christ as his Saviour, and then show him that the Bible is God's Word to him, and that the only way to be strong and grow in grace is to study the Word. I would then explain to him some simple method of Bible study and set him at it. The best way for a converted person to become interested in the study of the Bible is to get to actually studying it. The more one studies it the more his taste for Bible study increases.

16

What six books of the Bible should a young convert read or study first?

First of all, the Gospel of John. It is one of the profoundest books in the Bible, and yet there is much in it for the youngest believer. It was written for the specific purpose of bringing people to believe that Jesus is the Christ, the Son of God, that believing they might have life through His name (John 20:31), and there is nothing that the young believer needs more than to come to an intelligent, fixed faith in Jesus as the Christ, the Son of God.

After reading the Gospel of John, I would have the young disciple read the Gospel of Mark, then Luke, then Matthew. After this I would urge him to study the Acts of the Apostles, then the Epistle to the Romans. I think after that I would set him to reading the whole New Testament through in the order of the books.

Do you consider the Revised Version more correct than the Authorized?

As a rule the Revised Version is a more accurate rendering of the original than the Authorized, but there are some glaring exceptions to the contrary. A majority vote was taken in the committee of translation in order to reach a decision, where the translators differed.

What is your advice regarding the value and the use of the American Standard Bible in general work?

I think it is the opinion of the majority of Biblical scholars that the American Revision is upon the whole the most accurate rendering into English of the original Hebrew of the Old Testament and the original Greek of the New. However, it does not differ in many very important points from the English Revision.

The American Standard Bible is not very much used in England. This is partly due, undoubtedly, to the fact that obstacles are in the way of its circulation over there. I think every student of the Bible should have a copy of the Ameri-

17

can Revision, and wish that it might come into common use. It is not, however, in common use, and the use of it with some people is confusing and necessitates explanations. The Authorized Version is a substantially accurate rendering of the original Scriptures, and as a rule I use it in dealing with inquirers, for the reason that they are likely to be familiar with the wording, and if I should happen to use a text in the American Revision that varied in a striking way from the Bible to which they had been accustomed from childhood, they might get to thinking about words instead of having their attention fixed upon the thought.

To me it is unfortunate that there are two revisions. It is to be greatly deplored that the two committees did not arrive at an agreement.

There are some verses in the Bible that are not translated the way you know that they were intended to be. When a man takes up those points with you, what do you tell him?

I tell him we know now what the correct translation is, and I show him what it is. There is not one fundamental doctrine that has been touched by the variations in manuscripts or in translations.

CARD-PLAYING

Is there any harm in a Christian playing a quiet game of cards at home?

Yes. If we are to enjoy the fullest blessing that is possible for us in Christ Jesus we must keep absolutely free from every questionable thing, and cards are certainly questionable. They are a gambler's chief weapon. More persons become gamblers through card-playing than in any other way. Thousands and tens of thousands of young men and women who started out playing cards without any thought that they would ever become gamblers have been sucked into this awful maelstrom through the growth of the card-playing mania. In countless instances the quiet family card table has proved to be the kindergarten for the gambling of hell. I knew a family where the boys were taught to play cards by their parents. Their parents proceeded upon the theory that home ought to be made so interesting that the boys would not care to go away from home at night. The home was indeed a pleasant home, and the theory worked very well for a while, but the time comes when boys do go away from home. There were three boys in this family. Two of them learned to play cards, the other one had no taste for them. When the time came for the family to break up and the boys to go out into the world, the two boys who had learned to play cards at home both became gamblers. This is only one instance among many. I could tell of young woman after young woman and young man after young man who would have recoiled from the thought of gambling when they began to play cards, but who afterward found themselves in social positions where they felt compelled to play—first for prizes, and then for money—and they fell victims to the awful gambling mania.

Matters are far worse in America today than they were years ago. Bridge-whist has wrought frightful inroads in our best families. There have been some appalling tragedies. Cards have brought immeasurable misery. They are a thoroughly unclean thing, and should be utterly renounced by every follower of Jesus Christ.

Furthermore, card-playing is a form of amusement which it is almost impossible to indulge in in moderation. With almost every one that plays cards card-playing becomes almost a mania. Middle aged men who play cards are soon putting time into card-playing that ought to be put into business or into moral and spiritual culture. Women that get to card-playing soon put time into the cards that they ought to be putting into the care of their families and into the improvement of their minds. Young men and young women who get to playing cards put time into it that they ought to put into study and into preparation for larger usefulness. I could tell many instances that have come under my own personal observation of women who have neglected their home and children for cards, of men who have neglected their business,

19

and of young men and young women who have neglected study. Card-playing is like drinking. One may drink wine moderately, but the overwhelming probability in our land and day is that if he gets to drinking wine at all he will get to drinking immoderately. It is almost certain that if one gets to playing cards he will soon do it immoderately. It is not merely a fascinating game, it is an intoxicating and therefore perilous amusement.

Besides all this, even if one should play cards without bringing injury to themselves they will bring harm to others. Young men and young women seeing a Christian playing cards will be encouraged to play them, and while the Christian may himself remain a moderate player all his days some of those who have been emboldened to play through his example will surely become immoderate players and eventually gamblers. Here is a place where the words of the apostle Paul apply with great force: "It is good not to eat flesh, nor to drink wine, nor to do anything whereby thy brother stumbleth" (Romans 14:21, R. V.), and his other words in I Corinthians 8:13, R. V.: "If meat maketh my brother to stumble I will eat no flesh for evermore, that I make not my brother to stumble."

THE CHRISTIAN LIFE

What advice do you give for making a success of the Christian life?

There are seven steps in the path marked out in the Bible.

1. *Begin right.* What a right beginning is we see in John 1:12: "But as many as *received Him,* to them gave He power to become the sons of God, even to them that believe on His name."

Receive Christ as your Saviour who died for your sin. Trust the whole matter of your forgiveness to Him. Rest upon the fact that He has paid the full penalty of your sin. "For He hath made Him to be sin for us, who knew no sin; that we might be made the righteousness of God in Him" (II Corinthians 5:21).

20

Take Him as your Deliverer, who will save you from the power of sin, who will quicken you when dead in trespasses and sins. Don't try to save yourself from the power of sin. Trust Him to do it.

Take Him as your Master. Don't seek to guide your own life. Surrender unconditionally to His lordship over you. It is a joyous life all along the way, the life of entire surrender. If you have never done it before and wish to make a success of the Christian life, go alone with God, get down on your knees, and say: *"All* for Jesus."

2. *Confess Christ openly before men.* Matthew 10:32: "Whosoever therefore shall confess Me before men, him will I confess also before My Father which is in heaven." Romans 10:10: "For with the heart man believeth unto righteousness, and with the mouth confession is made unto salvation." The life of confession is the life of full salvation.

3. *Study the Word.* I Peter 2:2 "As newborn babes desire the sincere milk of the Word, that ye may grow thereby." The Word of God is the soul's food. It is the nourishment of the new life. One who neglects the Word cannot make much of a success of the Christian life. All who get on in the Christian life are great feeders on the Word of God.

4. *Pray without ceasing* (I Thessalonians 5:17). The one who would succeed in the Christian life must lead a life of prayer. That is easy enough if you only set about it.

Have set times for prayer. The rule of David and Daniel, three times a day, is a good rule: "Evening and morning and at noon will I pray, and cry aloud: and He shall hear my voice" (Psalm 55:17); "Now when Daniel knew that the writing was signed, he went into his house: and his windows being open in his chamber toward Jerusalem he kneeled upon his knees three times a day, and prayed, and gave thanks before his God, as he did aforetime" (Daniel 6:10). Begin the day with thanksgiving and prayer for the definite needs of the present day. Stop in the midst of the bustle and worry and temptation of the day for thanksgiving and prayer. Close the day with thanksgiving and prayer.

Then there should be the special prayer in special temptation—when we see the temptation approaching. Keep looking to God. It is not needful to be on our knees all of the time But the *heart* should be on its knees all the time.

There are three things I think the one who would make a success of the Christian life must especially pray. First, for wisdom—"If any of you lack wisdom, let him ask of God" (James 1: 5); second, for strength—"They that wait upon the Lord shall renew their strength" (Isaiah 40:31); third, for the Holy Spirit—"Your heavenly Father shall give the Holy Spirit to them that ask Him" (Luke 11:13). If you have not yet received the baptism with the Holy Spirit you should offer definite prayer for this definite blessing and definitely expect to receive it. If you have already received the baptism with the Holy Spirit you should with each new emergency of Christian work pray to God for a new filling with the Holy Spirit (Acts 4:31).

5. *Go to work for Christ.* Matthew 25:29: "For unto every one that hath shall be given, and he shall have abundance; but from him that hath not shall be taken away even that which he hath." The context means that those who use what they have will get more, and those that let what they have lie idle will lose even that. The working Christian, the one who uses his talents, whether few or many, in Christ's service, is the one who gets on in the Christian life here, and who will hereafter hear the "Well done, thou good and faithful servant, enter thou into the joy of thy Lord."

Find some work to do for Christ and do it. *Seek* for work. If it is nothing more than distributing tracts or invitations do it. Always be looking for something more to do *for* Christ, and you will always be receiving something more *from* Christ.

6. *Give liberally.* Proverbs 11:25: "The liberal soul shall be made fat"; II Corinthians 9:6, 8: "He which soweth sparingly shall reap also sparingly, and he which soweth bountifully shall reap also bountifully. And God is able to make all grace abound toward you, that ye, always having all sufficiency in all things, may abound to every good work." Success and growth in Christian life depend on few things more than upon liberal giving. A stingy Christian cannot be

22

a growing Christian. It is wonderful how a Christian man begins to grow when he begins to give.

7. *Keep pushing on.* "Brethren, I count not myself to have apprehended: but this one thing I do, forgetting those things which are behind, and reaching forth unto those things which are before, I press toward the mark for the prize of the high calling of God in Christ Jesus" (Philippians 3:13, 14).

Forget the sins which lie behind. If you fail anywhere, if you fall, don't be discouraged, don't give up, don't brood over the sin. Confess it instantly. Believe God's Word: "If we confess our sins He is faithful and just to forgive us our sins, and to cleanse us from all unrighteousness" (I John 1:9). Believe the sin is forgiven, forget it, press on. Satan beguiles many a poor soul here. He keeps us brooding over our failures and sins.

Forget the achievements and victories of the past, and press on to greater victories. Satan cheats many of us out of the larger life. He keeps us thinking so much of what we have already obtained, and makes us so contented with it, and so puffed up over it, that we come to a standstill, or even backslide. Our only safety is in forgetting those things which are behind, and pressing on. There is always something better ahead until we "come . . . unto a perfect man, unto the measure of the stature of the fulness of Christ" (Ephesians 4:13).

CHRISTIAN SCIENCE

How would you prove the error of Christian Science?

Many in our day are being led astray into Christian Science. Most Christian Scientists claim to believe the Bible. Take them, therefore, to I John 4:1-3:

"Beloved, believe not every spirit, but try the spirits, whether they are of God: because many false prophets are gone out into the world of God. Hereby know we the spirit: every spirit that confesseth that Jesus Christ is come in the flesh is of God, and every spirit that confesseth not that Jesus Christ is come in the flesh is not of God. And this is that

23

spirit of antichrist, whereof ye have heard that it should come, and even now already is it in the world."

Note this passage in relation to the very foundation of Christian Science, which denies as one of its fundamental postulates the reality of matter, the reality of the body, and (of necessity) the reality of the incarnation. Show them by this passage that the Bible says that every spirit that confesses not Jesus Christ is come in flesh is not of God, but of antichrist, and so not "Christian."

Why do you believe the claim of Mrs. Eddy to have received the tenets of Christian Science by divine inspiration to be false?

First of all, because it has been proved that she got her theories from a man by whom she was treated; that in writing her first book in its original form she did not claim it was original or received from God, but that she was writing down the views frankly confessed of this person by whom she had been treated and under whom she studied.

In the second place, I know the claim that she received the tenets of Christian Science from God is false because the tenets themselves are false. Mrs. Eddy denies the reality of the incarnation, and this is one of the primary tests of the truth or falsity of any system or doctrine, the decisive question to ask of any spirit and any system of doctrines, as shown in the previous question. Mrs. Eddy also denies the atonement, the fundamental truth of the Gospel. Her view of the atonement is not the one taught in the Bible, namely, that Jesus Christ Himself bore our sins in His own body on the cross (I Peter 2:24; II Cor. 5:21; Gal. 3:13). These are only some of the many great errors in the teaching of Mrs. Eddy.

There are, it is true, some elements of truth in the teachings of Christian Science. Every false system must have some true teachings in it, otherwise it could not be made to go at all. Every dangerous system of error takes some truth and distorts and perverts it and covers it up with a mass of error. That the mind has a tremendous influence over the body and that much disease can be overcome through the mind is unquestionably true. That God answers prayer and in answer to prayer heals the sick is taught in the Bible and taught by experience. That Jesus Christ had a mission for the body as well as for the soul is clearly taught in Scripture, and that a great deal of harm has been done by the use of drugs every wise physician admits. Mrs. Eddy has taken these truths, which the church oftentimes has lost sight of, and starting out with these truths has made an open door for the introduction of a vast amount of destructive and damning error. If the church had been truer to its own mission and given to men a real and full and satisfying Gospel, the great majority of those who have fallen a prey to Mrs. Eddy would have escaped the snare.

THE CHURCH

What are the conditions of entrance into the church?

The word "church" in the New Testament is used, first, of the whole body of believers in Jesus Christ (Matthew 16:18; Acts 20:28: 2:47; Ephesians 5:24, 25; Colossians 1:18, 24). Second, it is used of the body of believers in any place, as (for example) the church of the Thessalonians (I Thessalonians 1:1). Third, it is used of the local congregations meeting regularly for the breaking of bread and worship and teaching as (for example) the church that met in Rome in the home of Priscilla and Aquila (Romans 16:5).

The conditions of entrance into the church in its first and deeper meaning are acceptance of Jesus Christ as one's personal Saviour, surrender to Him as Lord and Master, and open confession of Him before the world (Acts 2:38, 41, 47).

The conditions of entrance into local churches are determined by the churches themselves. Most churches receive members upon satisfactory evidence that they have really forsaken sin, accepted Christ as their personal Saviour, and surrendered their lives to Him. Some churches require subscriptions to a creed more or less full. All the evangelical churches except the Friends require water baptism on the part of the applicant for membership, either as an infant or an adult.

What should an earnest Christian do when the churches are so full of worldliness and error as they are today? Should he join the church?

Yes. I fully recognize the worldliness that there is in many churches today, and the error that is taught from many a pulpit; but after all is said the church is the best organization there is in the world. What would the world be today if it were not for the churches which are in it? The churches even with all their present imperfections are the institutions that are saving society from utter corruption.

Any Christian can accomplish more for the salvation of souls and the upbuilding of Christian character and the good of the community by uniting with some church than he can by trying to live a Christian life by himself.

There may be times when one has to utter his protest against sins of a glaring character in some individual church, and when that protest will not be heard, and when it may be necessary for him to withdraw as a testimony against that church. But these occasions are comparatively rare.

Great corruption—unspeakable immorality, in fact—had crept into the church in Corinth, and yet Paul did not hint for a moment to any of the members of that church that they should withdraw from it. He did write them to judge the evil and put it away, but not a suggestion that they should withdraw. Even Jesus did not withdraw from the synagogues of His day until He was put out. Synagogue worship had become full of formality and error, and yet it was the custom of our Lord to attend the synagogue on the sabbath day (Luke 4:16). The apostle Paul followed His example in this matter (Acts 17:2).

There are many earnest Christian men and women today who have lost all power and influence for God and good in the community by coming out of their fellowship with other believers who were not as well instructed as they, and by giving themselves up to harsh and censorious criticism.

Of course, if the pastor of a church persistently preaches glaring and pernicious error, one should enter his protest against it and should not allow his children to sit under that kind of false doctrine.

It is true that in the Book of Revelation men are bidden to come out of Babylon, but Babylon is not yet formed. Everything in the Book of Revelation after the fourth chapter and first verse describes the time after the rapture of the Church, not the present time, and it is handling the Word of God deceitfully and not rightly dividing the Word of truth to apply this command to come out of Babylon to the present time and the present state of the churches.

Do you believe in having different denominations?
Do sects do more harm than good in the cause of religion?

Undoubtedly *sects* do more harm than good in the cause of religion, for the very thought of sect is of something that makes division. The animating spirit of the sect is division.

But a *denomination* is not necessarily a sect. The different denominations have arisen because different persons saw some truths very clearly that others did not see, and around these persons other people have gathered to enforce that particular phase of truth. For example the Congregationalists and the Presbyterians arose in England and Scotland to stand for the truth of the liberty of the individual believer. Many other truths were associated with this in the development of these denominations. The Quakers arose to stand for the truth of the illumination and guidance of the Holy Spirit for the individual believer today. The Methodists arose to stand for the truth of definite personal experience of regeneration and the necessity of a holy life. Afterward other truths, such as the freedom of the will, became prominently associated with these in the teaching of the Methodist denomination. By standing strongly for some neglected truths that needed to be emphasized the denominations have doubtless done good. In the present imperfect state of man, where no individual is large enough to take in the whole scope of God's truth, and where one man sees one line of truth strongly and another man another line of truth, denominations have been necessary. But it is well that denominational lines are now fast sinking out of sight and each denomination is coming to understand and accept the truths for which other denominations have stood.

What do you think of the institutional church? Is it not detrimental to the real work of the church as set forth in the New Testament?

By an institutional church I understand a church that not only does the direct work of preaching the Gospel and building Christians up by teaching the Bible, but a church that also looks after the physical and mental welfare of its members and congregation by various institutions. Such work is not necessarily detrimental to the real work of the church as set forth in the New Testament. It may be a valuable auxiliary, provided that the physical and intellectual are kept in thorough subordination to the spiritual.

The apostolic church was in a measure an institutional church. It looked out for the physical welfare of its members, all property was held in common (Acts 2:44, 45; 4:34, 35; 6:1-4), and the Word of God increased and prospered under these circumstances (Acts 2:47; 4:4; 5:14; 6:7). Of course, the institutions were not many, nor very largely developed. In a similar way today the church can have various institutions for looking after the physical and intellectual welfare of its members. If it is located among the poor it can have savings institutions, a society for buying coal at the cheapest rate, libraries, educational classes, and so forth, and accomplish a vast amount of good, and make all this subservient to the preaching of the Gospel. All these things can be used as means of getting hold of men, women and children and bringing them to saving knowledge of Jesus Christ.

But there is always a danger in an institutional church. The danger is that the institutions get to be the main thing and the Gospel be put in a secondary place, or altogether lost sight of. This has been the history of more than one institutional church in this country, and it is always a danger. In such a case the institutional church becomes detrimental to the real work of the church as set forth in the New Testament. The first work of the church is seeking and saving the lost. (Luke 19:10; Matthew 5:19), its second work is feeding the flock (Acts 20:28; I Peter 5:2), and its third work is training the membership for intelligent service (Ephesians 4:11, 12, R. V.). If the institutions connected with the church are allowed to put any one of these three things in the background, they do more harm than good, but if the institutions are carried on in the spirit of prayer and with the intention, never lost sight of for a moment, of winning men for Christ, and everything is made subordinate to the preaching of the Gospel and the salvation of the lost and the edification of the saints, the institutions may be very helpful.

But the more experience I have with churches and ministers the more the feeling grows on me that the church that is needed today is not so much the institutional church as the evangelistic church.

Is it ever right to ask unconverted though moral people to teach a Sunday school class or do other definite Christian work in the church?

"Ever" is a pretty comprehensive word. The ideal way is to have only thoroughly regenerated and spiritually minded people to teach a Sunday school class or to sing in a choir. The church with which I am connected takes the ground that the very first condition of admission to membership in our choir is that the person applying should give good evidence of being born again. The second condition is that they have a voice for singing. But I can conceive of conditions where it would be warranted to set an unconverted person to teach a Sunday school class. For example, if I should go into a mining town where there was no Sunday school and no religious work of any kind, if I could start a Sunday school

29

there before I left the town and get some moral person to teach the Bible, *if there was no regenerated person to get,* I believe I would start the school and trust that the Spirit of God would use the Scripture as a blessing to both the teacher and the taught. I would take the appointment of this person as a teacher as an opportunity to urge upon him the necessity of a personal acceptance of Christ.

In holding our meetings around the world the committee that organized the choirs often received persons that I do not believe were really converted, and I have used the fact that they were in the choir as an opportunity of getting at them, and hundreds of persons have thus been converted to God.

What authority is there for or against women being prominent in church work?

There is no authority in the Bible for a woman to have the place of supremacy in the church. When she takes it she steps out of her right place. She goes against the plain teaching of the Bible when she takes the place of the authoritative teacher in the church (I Timothy 2:12).

But there is abundant Bible warrant for her being active and (in that sense) prominent in church work. Women were the first divinely commissioned preachers of the risen Christ. Jesus Christ Himself sent them to declare His resurrection to the men disciples (John 20:17, 18; Matthew 28:9, 10). Women were endued by God with prophetical gifts (Acts 21:9). In the very chapter in the Bible in which women are forbidden to do idle talking and asking questions in the church there are directions as to how a woman should prophesy, that is, how she should speak in the power of the Spirit (I Corinthians 11:5). The apostle Paul speaks of the women who had labored with him in the Gospel (Philippians 4:3). There is plain indication that Priscilla was more gifted than her husband Aquila. She was associated with her husband in taking the preacher Apollos aside and expounding unto him the way of God more carefully (Acts 18:26), and her name is mentioned first (see R. V.).

What is the Scriptural means of raising money for church or other Christian uses?

By the free will offerings of saved people, each one laying aside in store on the first day of the week a definite proportion of his income (I Corinthians 16:2).

Certainly it is not the Scriptural way of raising money to raise it by fairs, bazaars or any other method that reduces the church of Christ to the level of the vaudeville entertainment. These methods are unwise even from a business standpoint, and they certainly are dishonoring to Jesus Christ. Those are the successful churches that step out in obedience to the Word of God and depend upon the freewill offerings of the people, and they soon find they have more money for their own work and more money for foreign missions than those churches have that stoop to dishonor their Lord by raising money in such a way as makes the church a reproach even among people of the world.

Would you ask an unsaved person to contribute money or goods for the support or benefit of church work?

No, I would not. God is not dependent upon His enemies for the carrying on of His work. God's work should be supported by the glad freewill offerings of His own people, as explained in the previous answer.

Furthermore, when unsaved people give to the support of God's work it frequently acts as a salve to their conscience, and it makes them harder to reach. They say: "I am supporting the church," and many of them hope to get to heaven that way.

Of course, if some unsaved person of his own volition should see fit to put money into the contribution box, or something of that kind, I would hesitate to insult him or take the responsibility of refusing his money, but I should let it be distinctly understood in taking collections that it was not the money but the souls of the unsaved we were after and that men should give themselves first to the Lord before they gave their money.

31

THE COMING AGAIN OF JESUS CHRIST

Does the Bible teach that Jesus Christ is coming back to this earth personally and visibly?

It does. There is nothing more clearly taught in the Bible than that Jesus Christ is coming back to this earth personally, bodily and visibly. In Acts 1:11 the two men in white apparel who sood by the disciples as they gazed steadfastly into heaven after Jesus as He was taken up before their eyes, said: "This same Jesus which was received up from you into heaven shall *so come in like manner as ye have seen Him go into heaven.*" Now they had seen Him going into heaven personally, bodily, visibly, and they were told He was to come back just as He had gone.

An attempt has been made by those who deny the personal return of our Lord to say that "in like manner" means "with equal certainty," but the Greek words translated "so in like manner" permit of no such construction. They are never so used. Literally translated they mean "thus in the manner which," and are never used as describing anything but the manner, the precise manner, in which the thing is done. Jesus Christ is coming back exactly as the disciples saw Him going, personally, bodily, visibly.

The same truth is taught in John 14:3; I Thessalonians 4:16, 17; and many other passages. In Hebrews 9:28 we are told: "So Christ was offered to bear the sins of many, and unto them that *look for Him* shall He *appear the second time* without sin unto salvation." The word which in this passage is translated "shall appear" translated literally would be "shall be seen." It is a word only used of seeing with the eye. In Revelation 1:7 we read: "Behold, *He cometh* with clouds, and *every eye shall see Him,* and they also which bruised Him, and all kindreds of the earth shall wail because of Him."

These very plain promises cannot by any fair system of interpretation be made to refer to the coming of Christ in the

32

Holy Spirit, as some would say. The coming of the Holy Spirit is in a very real sense the coming of Christ (see John 14:15-18, 21-23). But it is not the coming referred to in these passages, and cannot be made such except by perverting the plain words of God.

Nor is the coming described in these passages the coming of Christ to receive the believer at the time of his death. The details given do not fit the death of the believer.

Neither do these passages refer to the coming of Christ at the destruction of Jerusalem. The destruction of Jerusalem was in a sense a precursor, prophecy and type of the judgment at the end of the age, and therefore in Matthew 24 and Mark 13 the two events so described are in connection with each other. But God's judgment on Jerusalem is manifestly not the event referred to in the passage above given. After the coming of the Holy Spirit at Pentecost, and after the destruction of Jerusalem, the coming again of Jesus Christ, which is so frequently mentioned in the New Testament, is the great hope of the church, and is still mentioned as lying in the future. (See, for example, John 21:22,23; Revelation 1:7; 22:20).

How is Jesus Christ coming again?

As already said, He is coming personally, visibly and bodily. But further than this, He is coming with great publicity (Matthew 24:26, 27; Revelation 1:7). Every now and then some one appears in some corner of the earth who is announced to be Christ in His second coming, but these "inner chamber" Christs and "obscure corner" Christs are a humbug long since predicted and exploded. Christ is coming in the clouds of heaven with power and great glory (Matthew 24: 30). He is coming in the glory of His Father with the holy angels (Matthew 16:27; Mark 8:38; II Thessalonians 1:7, R.V.). He is coming unannounced, without warning, unexpectedly, suddenly (Revelation 16:15; I Thessalonians 5:2, 3; Matthew 24:37-39; Luke 21:34, 35).

Do you believe that the second coming of Christ is near at hand? If so, why? What should we do to prepare for Him?

As far as I know our Lord may return again any day. There is no event predicted in Scripture that must occur before Jesus comes to receive His own to Himself, although it seems as if there are some events that must occur before He comes to the earth with His saints (II Thessalonians 2:2-4, 8). As far as we know He may come for us believers at any moment, and He Himself has bidden us to be always ready because in such an hour as we think not He is coming again (Matthew 24:44).

Furthermore, there seems to be indications that His coming draweth nigh. II Timothy 3:1-5 gives a very accurate description of our own time. The increase of unbelief in the professing church and in the pulpit, the growing unrest in the social and political world, the apparently rapid development of the Antichrist—all these things seem to point to the near approach of our Lord. But we should bear in mind that earnest men of God and students of the Bible have often thought in times past that the coming of the Lord was very near, and it was, and they were not mistaken. Those that thought it was so far away that they allowed it to have no effect upon their lives were the ones who were really mistaken.

Today men's hearts are "failing them for fear" and "for expectation of things which are coming on the world" (Luke 21:26, R. V.). But when the true believer and intelligent student of the Word sees these things begin to come to pass he will not be discouraged, but will look up and lift up his head because he knows that his redemption draweth nigh (Luke 21:28). We should all let our loins be girded about and our lights be burning, and we should be like unto men that wait for their lord when he returns from the wedding, that when He does come and knock we may open unto Him immediately (Luke 12:35, 36).

What is the logical and adequate explanation of Matthew 16:28, where Jesus said: "Verily I say unto you, There be

some standing here which shall not taste of death till they see the Son of man coming in His kingdom"?

The answer to this question is evident if one reads right on, ignoring the chapter division between the 16th and 17th chapters of Matthew. This division is not a part of the original Scriptures, but an editor's addition, and sometimes the division is made in an illogical way—noticeably so in this case.

After quoting the words in question Matthew goes on to describe the transfiguration of Christ. In this transfiguration Jesus, the Son of man, was seen "coming in His kingdom." He was manifested in the glory that is properly His. If things had taken their natural course He would then and there have been glorified without passing through death, but He turned His back upon that glory and went down from the mountain to meet the awful tragedy of His death, the only way in which He could redeem men. It was of His decease (atoning death) that Moses and Elijah spoke with Him when they appeared with Him in the glory (Luke 9:31). This transfiguration, beheld by some who were standing with Him when He uttered the words found in Matthew 16:28, was the Son of man seen coming in His kingdom.

CONFESSION OF SINS

Ought we to confess our sins to man, or only to God?

First of all, we should confess them to God. David says in Psalm 32:5: "I acknowledge my sin unto *Thee* (that is, the Lord), and mine iniquity have I not hid. I said: 'I will confess my transgression *unto the Lord,*' and Thou forgavest the iniquity of my sin." In I John 1:9 we read: "If we confess our sins (and it evidently means, *unto God*) He is faithful and just to forgive us our sins and to cleanse us from all unrighteousness."

If we have sinned against man, I believe we should confess our sins to the man against whom we have sinned. We should be reconciled to our brother who has aught against us (Matthew 5:23, 24). It is well also to confess our sins one to another in order that we may pray one for another (James 5:16). There is not the slightest hint, however, that this means that we should confess our sins to a priest any more than to any other brother. It says: "Confess one to another," and there is no more reason why we should confess our sins to a priest than that the priest should confess his sins to us.

If we have sinned publicly we should make public confession of our sins. But there is nothing in the Bible to indicate that one should make a detailed public confession of all his transgressions, or even that he should confess to any man every sin that he has committed. Religious impostors often require this of their disciples, and in this way they get a hold over their disciples and rule them by fear of exposure. One of the best known religious impostors of modern times got a hold upon his people in this way. He made them confess everything mean and vile that they had done, then he terrorized them, got their money from them, made slaves of them. There are some things that a man should keep to himself and God.

CONSCIENCE AS GUIDE

Is conscience a sufficient guide for man?

No. Conscience, using the word in the sense of the moral intuition that every man possesses that right is right and wrong is wrong, and that we each of us ought to take our stand upon the right to follow it wherever it carries us, is sufficient to lead us to an absolute surrender to do the right whatever it may be, but then there comes the question of what is right. Conscience, in the sense of moral judgment as to what is right or wrong, is certainly not a sufficient guide to man. Many men do conscientiously things that are utterly wrong because their moral judgment has been improperly educated. Conscience needs to be enlightened as to what is right by divine revelation and by the personal illumination of the Holy Spirit.

If we surrender ourselves to do the right wherever it carries us, and make an honest search for the right and the true,

36

we shall be led to see that Jesus Christ is the Son of God and a teacher sent from God (John 7:17), and then we will bring our moral judgment to Him for education. Having accepted Jesus Christ as the Son of God and a teacher sent from God, we will be logically led by the study of His Word to accept the entire Bible as the Word of God, and will consequently take it as our guide in conduct. Furthermore, we will be led to see that it is our privilege to be taught of the Holy Spirit and to be guided into right conduct by Him.

CONSECRATION

What is meant by consecration? How often should a person consecrate himself?

In modern use (which, by the way, is not the Bible use) the word "consecration" means the surrendering of one's self and all that one has wholly to God. The word "sanctify" as used in the Bible has practically the same meaning when applied to sanctifying ourselves. It means to set apart for God.

Every Christian should consecrate himself once for all to God. He should put into God's hands all that he is and all that he has, for God to use him and his as He will, to send him where He will and do with him what He will. Having thus consecrated himself he should never take himself out of God's hands. But many do consecrate themselves to God and afterward go back on their consecration, as Samson did, and are shorn of their strength, as Samson was. In such a case a man should re-consecrate himself to God, and even where a man has not taken back his consecration it is a good thing to constantly re-acknowledge it in order that one may keep it distinctly in mind.

Furthermore, consecration gets a deeper significance the longer we live. At one time of our life we may give ourselves up wholly to God as far as we understand it at the time, but as we study the Word and grow in grace consecration will ever gain a deeper meaning. I believe I have been wholly

God's for many years, but only yesterday I got a deeper understanding of what it means to be wholly God's than I have ever had before.

CONVICTION OF SINS

How is conviction of sin produced?

What character of preaching would you advise to bring to the people a realization of the awfulness of sin, and to bring upon them conviction of and for sin?

The law was given to bring men to a knowledge of sin (Romans 3:20), and I find that the preaching of the law does bring men to such a knowledge. I preach on the Ten Commandments, looking to the Holy Spirit to show men how they have not kept them. I also preach on Matthew 7:12, the so-called Golden Rule, to show people they have not kept that and therefore cannot be saved by the Golden Rule: "All things whatsoever ye would that men should do to you, do you even so to them." I preach on Matthew 22:37, 38, and by the use of these verses seek to show people that they have not only sinned but they have broken the first and greatest of God's commandments: "Jesus said unto him: Thou shalt love the Lord thy God with all thy heart, and with all thy soul, and with all thy mind. This is the first and great commandment."

But we read in John 16:9 that the sin of which the Holy Spirit convicts men is the sin of unbelief in Jesus Christ, and we see in Acts 2:37 (compared with the words of Peter that precede) that the sin of which the Holy Spirit convicted so many thousands on the day of Pentecost was the sin of rejecting Jesus Christ. Working along this line I find that holding up before men the majesty and glory of Jesus Christ and the sacrifice He made for us, then driving home the awfulness of the sin of rejecting such a Saviour, brings the deepest conviction of sin.

But in all our preaching we must bear in mind that it is the Holy Spirit, not we ourselves, who convicts men of sin.

He does it through the truth that we present, but we must realize our dependence upon Him and look to Him and count on Him to do the work. Here is where many make a mistake. They try to convict men of sin instead of putting themselves in such an attitude toward the Holy Spirit that He will convict men through them.

DANCING

Where does it say in the Bible that dancing is a sin?

It does not say anywhere in the Bible that dancing is a sin. Dancing is not a sin. Dancing is perfectly proper in its place. It is an expression of joy, even sometimes of religious joy. Miriam the prophetess and the women who were with her danced in their joy over their deliverance from the Egyptians (Exodus 15:20), and God seems to have been pleased. David danced before the ark. There is a time to dance. There is no wrong whatever in dancing in the proper time and in the proper way.

But mixed dancing, the dancing of men with women in the way in which it is carried on today even in the most select dancing parties, permits a familiarity of contact between the sexes that is nowhere else allowed in decent society. It is the cause of untold sin and misery. It is forbidden in II Corinthians 6:17, R. V., where we are told to touch no unclean thing—and the modern mixed dance is unquestionably an unclean thing. It is immodest, impure, unwholesome.

Is it right for a Christian to dance?

It is not right for a Christian to do anything that will bring reproach upon the cause of Christ or in any wise lessen his or her own influence for Christ. One can imagine conditions under which a Christian could engage in a square dance without bringing reproach on the cause of Christ, but the question is not what are the conditions that we can imagine but what are the conditions that actually exist today. It is impossible under existing conditions for any Christian to

39

dance without bringing reproach upon the cause of Christ or without lessening his or her own influence for Christ.

In the dance as it exists today in America and in England a familiarity of contact is permitted between the sexes that is nowhere else permitted in decent society. This is true in the most select dances that are held. If any lady should permit any gentleman except her husband, father or brother, to handle her any where else as he handles her on the dancing floor she would be regarded as immodest and unwomanly, if nothing worse. Certainly these attitudes do not become any better when taken accompanied by strains of seductive music, and by movements which have beyond a question a morally deleterious effect upon many that engage in them. I have no doubt that many a pure girl engages in the modern dance without evil thoughts, but I know that many of the men, probably the overwhelming majority who dance with her, do have evil thoughts. The hardest fight that the young man of today has on hand is the fight for purity in thought and act, and there is scarcely any other institution known to modern society that makes the fight for purity in thought and act so hard for the young man as the modern dance. If modest young women could hear the young men who dance with them in the most select parties talk afterward among themselves I feel confident that no self-respecting young woman would ever engage in the dance again. These are not pleasant facts to contemplate, but they are facts, and we ought to face them.

Furthermore, the Christian young woman who dances loses her influence with many of those whom she desires to win for Christ. While the world constantly seeks to allure believers into compromise with itself, and oftentimes praises them for liberality and breadth of thought if they do indulge with them in their questionable pastimes, nevertheless at heart the world despises a compromising Christian.

Further still, the dance interferes with the love of Bible study, the love of secret prayer, the love of service for Christ. It does not help but hinders the spiritual life in all directions. No Christian can dance without suffering for it beyond description, and without bringing reproach on the cause of Christ. Every true Christian desires for himself the highest possible spiritual attainment, he will be satisfied with nothing less. The dance beyond a question interferes with such attainment.

DEITY OF JESUS CHRIST

How would you prove that Jesus Christ is really the Son of God?

First of all, I would prove that *He rose from the dead.* Of this there is abundant proof.[1] The fact that Jesus Christ rose from the dead proves beyond a question that He is the Son of God.

When He was here upon earth *He repeatedly declared* that He was the Son of God, the Son of God in a unique sense, the Son of God in a sense in which no other man is the Son of God. In Mark 12:6 He taught that while the prophets, even the greatest of them, were servants, He was a Son, an only Son. In John 5:22, 23 He taught that all men should honor Him even as they honored the Father. In John 14:9 He went so far as to say: "He that hath seen Me hath seen the Father." Men hated Him for making this claim to be the Son of God, they put Him to death for making this claim (Matthew 26:63, 66), but before they put Him to death for making this claim He told them that God would set His seal to the claim by raising Him from the dead. It was a stupendous claim to make, it was an apparently absurd claim, but God did set His seal to it by raising Jesus from the dead. By doing this God Himself has said more clearly than if He should speak from the open heavens today:

"This Man is what He claims to be. He is My Son. All men should honor Him even as they honor the Father."

Jesus Christ proves Himself to be the Son of God by the claim He made to be the Son of God and by the way in which He substantiated that claim by His resurrection from the dead.

---

[1] Resurrection of the Human Body, Norman H. Camp (Moody Press).

But He also substantiated it by *His character*, by its beauty and strength and nobility. The character of Jesus Christ is well nigh universally admitted. Jews nowadays admit that. The most notorious infidels have admitted it. Even Col. Ingersoll once said:

"I wish to say once and for all, to that great and serene Man I gladly pay the homage of my admiration and my tears."

But here is this Man, whom all admit to be a good Man, a Man of honor and of truth and of nobility, claiming to be the Son of God. Certainly a Man of such character was what He claimed to be.

He substantiated His claim furthermore by *the miracles which He performed.* Herculean efforts have been put forth to discredit the Gospel stories of Christ's miracles, but these efforts have all resulted in utter and lamentable failure.

He substantiated His claim by *His influence* on the history of the world. It needs no argument to prove that Christ's influence upon the history of the world has been beneficent immeasurably beyond that of any other man who ever lived. His influence upon individual life, domestic life, social life, industrial life, political life, it would be foolish to compare with that of any other man, or that of all men put together. Now if Jesus Christ was not divine as He claimed to be, He was a blasphemer and an impostor or else a lunatic. It is easy to see that His influence upon history is not that of a lunatic, or that of a blasphemer and impostor. Then certainly He must have been the Son of God as He claimed.

I would furthermore prove that Jesus Christ is the Son of God by pointing to the fact that *He possesses divine power today.* It is not necessary to go back to the miracles Christ performed when upon earth to prove that He has divine power. He exercises that power today and any one can test it:

(1) He has *power to forgive sins.* Thousands can testify that they came to Christ burdened with an awful sense of guilt, and that He has actually given their guilty conscience peace, absolute peace;

(2) He has *power today to set Satan's victims free.* He sets the one chained by drink free from the power of drink, the one chained by opium free from the power of opium. You may say various cures do this, but the cases are not parallel. These various cures use drugs, Christ a mere word. Christ sets free not only from vices but from sin. He makes the impure man pure. He makes the selfish man unselfish, the devilish man Christlike. He re-creates men and women. The divine influence that Jesus Christ is exerting today over the lives of countless men and women proves beyond a peradventure that He is the Son of God. I know Jesus Christ is divine because of the divine work that He, and He alone has wrought in my own life.

DEPRAVITY OF MAN

· What do you mean by the doctrine of total depravity, and how would you prove it?

By the doctrine that man is totally depraved we do not mean that he is totally corrupt. The doctrine is that the will of the unregenerate man is set upon pleasing self and is therefore totally wrong, for it should be set upon pleasing God. The will that is not absolutely surrendered to God is turned the wrong way. But while seeking to please himself a man may do things that are morally attractive and beautiful. A man is not necessarily drawn to vicious and disgusting things. He prefers things that are high and noble and true, yet he may not prefer them because they are what God wills but because they are the things that attract him. He is as truly depraved as the man who chooses the vicious things, but his tastes are not as corrupt as those of the man who chooses vicious things. What every unregenerate man needs is a total turning around of his will, so that he no longer seeks to please himself but surrenders himself in all things to do the things that please God and because they please God.

We prove the doctrine of total depravity, first by the Scriptures. For example, Romans 8:7—"The carnal mind is enmity

43

against God, for it is not subject to the law of God, neither indeed can be"; Ephesians 4:18—"Having the understanding darkened, being alienated from the life of God through the ignorance that is in them because of the blindness of their heart"; Jeremiah 17:9—"The heart is deceitful above all things, and desperately wicked"; and many other Scriptures.

We prove it also by an appeal to facts. The picture of the unregenerate man given in the Scriptures at first sight seems to be too dark, but as we come to know men better—especially as we come to know ourselves better, and above all as we come to know God better and see ourselves in the light of His holiness—the Bible doctrine is found to be absolutely accurate.

THE DEVIL

Do you believe in a personal Devil?

Most assuredly I do. I could not believe in the Bible without believing in a personal Devil. I have conclusive proof that the Bible is the Word of God, therefore I believe what it teaches about the existence of a personal Devil.

In the account of the temptation of our Lord recorded in the Gospels of Matthew and Luke, we are distinctly told that the Devil (and the whole account evidently means a personal Devil) was the author of the temptations that came to our Lord (see Matthew 4:1-11; Luke 4:1-13). These accounts have no meaning if we try to make the Devil of the passage a mere figure of speech.

Furthermore, our Lord in the parable of the sower (in Matthew 13:1-23) distinctly teaches that there is a personal Devil. The Devil does not appear in the parable, where it might be explained as being figurative, but in the interpretation of the parable: "Then cometh the wicked one . . ." Now in parables we have figures, and in the interpretation of parables we have the literal facts for which the figures stand, so we have a literal Devil in the interpretation of this parable. It is only one of the numerous instances in which Jesus teaches the existence of a personal Devil.

44

Paul teaches the same, as (for example) in Ephesians 6:11, 12, R. V.: "Put on the whole armor of God, that ye may be able to stand against the wiles of the Devil. For our wrestling is not against flesh and blood, but against the principalities, against the powers, against the world-rulers of this darkness, against the spiritual hosts of wickedness in the heavenly places."

No rational interpretation of the Bible can interpret the Devil out of it. Any system of interpretation that does away with the Devil would do away with any doctrine which a man does not wish to believe.

But I also believe that there is a personal Devil because my own experience and observation teach me the existence of an unseen, very subtle, very cunning spirit of evil, who has domination over men throughout human society wherever found. The more I come in contact with men, the more I study history, and the more men open their hearts to me, the more firmly convinced I become that there is such a Devil as the Bible teaches that there is.

It is not pleasant to believe that there is a personal Devil, but the question is not what is pleasant to believe but what is true.

Why did God create Satan, or the Devil?

Because God is love. God created him whom we now call Satan as a being of very exalted glory. A hint of what Satan was as originally created we get in Ezekiel 28:12-15, R. V.:

"Thou sealest up the sum, full of wisdom, and perfect in beauty. Thou wast in Eden, the garden of God. Every precious stone wast thy covering. . . . The workmanship of thy tabrets and of thy pipes was in thee; in the day that thou wast created they were prepared. Thou wast the anointed cherub that covereth, and I have set thee so, so that thou wast upon the holy mountain of God. Thou hast walked up and down in the midst of the stones of fire. Thou wast perfect in thy ways from the day that thou wast created till unrighteousness was found in thee."

45

Because he was a being of such exalted glory he was a moral being, that is, a being with the power of choosing good or evil. He seems to have been the one that led the worship of the universe. But ambition entered his heart. He seems to have tried to direct to himself what properly belonged to God, and thus he fell. Falling from such a height he fell to the deepest depths and became that appalling being that he now is. The Devil of Scripture is not a hideous-looking being with horns and hoofs, but a being of very lofty intelligence who has turned his mighty powers to wrong and has thus become the great enemy of God and man.

Can God destroy Satan?

We do not know that it is taught anywhere in the Bible that God can destroy Satan, but God certainly can destroy or annihilate any beings that He has created if He sees fit. If He brought them into being He can put them out of being, otherwise God would not be omnipotent.

But it is clear from Scripture that to destroy Satan is not His will. Satan will exist and be tormented day and night forever and ever (Revelation 20:10).

If the question refers to Hebrews 2:14 the word "destroy" there means "bring to nought," not "annihilate" (see Revised Version).

Why does not God destroy Satan if He is omnipotent?

Because God has not yet worked out His purposes through Satan. Though Satan himself is evil God accomplishes His purposes of good through him. The day will come when we will understand what these purposes are, and will thank God even for Satan. God will make not only the wrath of man, but the wrath of Satan, to praise Him. The messenger of Satan that was sent to buffet Paul worked only good for Paul. He kept Paul from being exalted above measure (II Corinthians 12:7).

46

DIVORCE

Does the Bible permit a man under any circumstances to divorce his wife and marry another while the divorced wife is still living?

It is perfectly clear that the Bible does not permit of divorce and remarriage on any ground but one, and that whosoever puts away his wife, *saving for the cause of fornication,* "maketh her an adulteress" (Matthew 5:32), and that if he marries another he himself commits adultery (Matthew 19:9). This much is plain as day, namely that there is only one Scriptural ground for divorce and remarriage, namely, impurity on the part of the other party.

It is, however, objected to by some who hold that remarriage even on this ground is not permitted by Scripture; that in Romans 7:2, 3, it is stated *without any exception* that a woman who hath a husband is bound by the law to her husband so long as he liveth, and that if while her husband liveth she be married to another she should be called an adulteress. The answer to this seems evident, namely, that Paul in Romans 7 is not discussing the question of divorce but is simply using the matter of the marriage obligation as an illustration. The only point that illustrates is the point of death, and it would have been entirely out of his way to have gone into the matter of exceptions to the general law, as they had no bearing whatever on the question that he was discussing. The words of Christ seem to clearly imply that one may divorce his wife and marry another *in this one case* of infidelity, and be guiltless before God.

It would seem, however, that if one had contracted an unfortunate alliance of this kind, he would better remain single, at least until the death of the offending party, and thus avoid trouble in the flesh. But if one has divorced husband or wife on the ground of adultery and has already married another, there is no Scriptural reason why he or she should feel condemned.

ETERNAL PUNISHMENT

Do you believe in the eternal punishment of the wicked? What proof is there of eternal punishment?

We know nothing positively and absolutely about the future except what God Himself has been pleased to reveal in His Word. All beyond this is pure speculation, and man's speculations on such a subject are practically valueless. God knows all about the future, and God has been pleased to reveal some things that He knows about the future. On such a subject as this an ounce of God's revelation is worth tons of man's empty speculation. God has clearly revealed in the Bible the fact of eternal punishment for those who persist in sin and in the rejection of Jesus Christ, and this is conclusive proof of its reality. What the Bible says God says, and the Bible distinctly teaches the eternity of punishment of those who persistently reject the redemption that is in Christ Jesus, as (for instance):

Matthew 25:41, 46—"Depart from Me, ye cursed, into everlasting fire prepared for the Devil and his angels . . . These shall go away into everlasting punishment, but the righteous into life eternal"; Revelation 19:20; 20:10; 21:8—"And the beast was taken, and with him the false prophet that wrought miracles before him, with which he deceived them that had received the mark of the beast and them that worshipped his image. These both were cast alive into a lake of fire burning with brimstone. And the Devil that deceived them was cast into the lake of fire and brimstone where the beast and the false prophet are, and shall be tormented day and night for ever and ever. But the fearful, and unbelieving, and the abominable, and murderers, and whoremongers, and sorcerers, and idolaters, and all liars, shall have their part in the lake which burneth with fire and brimstone: which is the second death."

The expression "for ever and ever" used of the lake of fire prepared for the Devil and his angels, to which the persistently wicked also go, is used twelve times in the Book of Revelation. Eight times it refers to the duration of the existence or reign or glory of God and Christ, once to the duration of the blessed reign of the righteous, and in the three remaining instances to the duration of the torment of the Devil, the beast, the false prophet and the persistently wicked.

Does the Bible teach eternal torment for all of the unsaved? If so, where?

The Bible teaches in II Thessalonians 1:7-9 that when the Lord Jesus is revealed from heaven *all* those that know not God and obey not the Gospel of our Lord Jesus Christ shall be punished with everlasting destruction from the presence of the Lord, and from the glory of His power. The question then arises what does "destruction" mean. The Bible itself defines the term. We are told in Revelation 17:8, 11 that "the beast goeth into perdition." The word rendered "perdition" in both Authorized and Revised Versions, the same word which is elsewhere translated "destruction," is derived from the verb that is constantly translated "destroy." The word should therefore be translated "destruction" in this passage. So then if we can find out what the beast goeth into, we shall find out what "perdition" or "destruction" means. By turning to Revelation 19:20 we find that the beast was cast alive into the lake of fire burning with brimstone. Turning again to Revelation 20:10 we find that at the end of a thousand years after the beast was cast into the lake burning with brimstone the Devil was cast into the lake burning with fire and brimstone where the beast and the false prophet still are after a thousand years, and that they shall be "tormented day and night for ever and ever." So then this is what "destruction" means in Bible usage—"a portion in the lake of fire." Whether this is taken literally or figuratively it certainly means a condition of being in a place of conscious and unending torment.

How could a loving God create some of His creatures for eternal punishment?

God did not create any of His creatures for eternal punishment. God created all persons to love and obey Him, and to enjoy Him forever, but He created some of them as a higher order of beings with the capacity of choosing for themselves, good or evil. Some chose evil. But even then God did not abandon them, but made the greatest sacrifice in His power to save them from their own mad choice. He gave His Son to die for them, that repentance and forgiveness and life and glory might be possible for them. If men see fit not only to choose evil but having chosen evil to deliberately and persistently refuse the means of salvation which a loving God has provided for them at immeasurable cost to Himself, then their eternal punishment is their own fault, and to blame God for it is not only to be appallingly unjust but unpardonably ungrateful and unreasonable.

How can an infinitely holy and merciful God condemn creatures He loves to everlasting punishment?

It is not so much that God condemns any one to everlasting punishment as that men and women condemn themselves to everlasting torment by refusing the mercy and grace of God. Many men not only choose sin but they also choose to refuse the wonderfully gracious redemption from sin that God has provided. If men will not allow themselves to be saved from sin they must necessarily continue in it, and if they continue in it they must necessarily suffer torment as long as they continue in it. The time must come, sooner or later, when repentance becomes impossible, and so of course salvation becomes impossible. The everlasting torment which any one may endure will be simply the inevitable result of his own deliberate and persistent choice of sin.

Is it not unjust to punish a few years of sin with an eternity of torment?

The duration of the punishment of sin can never be determined by the time it takes to commit the sin. A man can kill another man in a few seconds, but a just penalty would be life-long imprisonment.

Furthermore, sin involves separation from God, and separation from God is torment. The torment must continue as long as the separation from God exists, and the separation from God must exist until sin is repented of and the Saviour accepted. The time must come when repentance and the acceptance of the Saviour become impossible, then one becomes eternally confirmed in his separation from God, and eternal torment must necessarily follow.

Further still, it is not a few years of sin that bring the eternity of punishment. A man may continue many years in sin and still escape eternal torment if he will only repent and accept Jesus Christ. It is the rejection of Jesus Christ that brings an eternity of torment. When we see sin in all its hideousness and enormity, the holiness of God in all its perfection, and the glory of Jesus Christ in all its infinity, nothing but a doctrine that those who persist in the choice of sin and who persist in the rejection of the Son of God, whom God in wonderful grace gave to die for our sins that we might have salvation—nothing but a doctrine that those who do this shall suffer eternal anguish will satisfy the demand of our own moral intuitions. Nothing but the fact that we dread suffering more than we hate sin and more than we love the glory of Jesus Christ, makes us repudiate the thought that beings who eternally choose sin should eternally suffer, or that men who despise God's mercy and spurn His Son should be given over to eternal anguish.

Would an earthly father consign his child to everlasting suffering? And if he would not, can we believe that God is as good as we are, and that He would treat His children in a way that we would not treat ours?

This question takes it for granted that all men are God's children. The Bible teaches that this is not true. All men are God's creatures and were created originally in His likeness, and in this sense they are all His offspring (Acts 17:26-

51

29), but men become God's children in the fullest sense by being born again of the Holy Spirit (John 3:3-6) through the personal acceptance of Jesus Christ as their Saviour (John 1:12; Galatians 3:26).

Second, God is something besides the Father even of believers. He is the moral governor of this universe. As a righteous moral governor of the universe He must punish sin, and if sin is eternally persisted in He must eternally punish it. Even a wise earthly father would separate one of his own children who persisted in sin from contact with his other children. If a man had a dearly beloved son who was a moral monster, he certainly would not allow him to associate with his daughters. If one whom you greatly loved should commit a gross wrong against someone you loved more, and should persist in it eternally, would you not consent to his eternal punishment?

Third, it is never safe to measure what an infinitely holy God would do by what we would do. As we look about us in the world today do we not see men and women suffering agonies that we would not allow our children to suffer if we could prevent it? What one of us could endure to see our children suffering some of the things that the men and women in the slums of the great city are suffering today? Why a God of love permits this to go on it may be difficult for us to explain, but that it does go on we know. What men and women suffer even in the life that now is as a result of their disobedience to God and their persistence in sin and their rejection of Jesus Christ ought to be a hint of what men will suffer in the eternal world if they go on in sin as the result of their having rejected the Saviour in the life that now is. It may sound well to say: "I believe in a God of love, and I do not believe that He will permit any of His creatures to go to an eternal hell," but if we open our eyes to the facts as they exist about us on every hand we will see how empty our speculations on this point are, for we do see even now this same God of love permitting many of His creatures to endure awful and ever-increasing agonies in the life that now is.

If any one is lost eternally, has not Satan then gained the victory over Christ, and is he not stronger than Christ?

No, Satan has gained no victory. It is not Satan who determines that one shall persist in sin, it is the individual himself. If he persists in sin Satan has gained no victory, and on the other hand Jesus Christ is not conquered. Jesus Christ will still be glorified, and God will be glorified. God's holiness is manifested and God Himself is glorified as truly in the punishment of the sinner as in the salvation of the believer. Righteous government here on earth is vindicated as truly when the offender is locked up in prison or executed as when the offender is brought to repentance.

Many seem to think that hell is a place ruled by Satan, but Satan does not rule there. Satan himself will be one of the prisoners, and the smoke of the torment of this persistent rebel against God arises for ever and ever as a testimony that God has conquered.

EXISTENCE OF EVIL

How can God permit evil to exist in the world?

When we enter the domain of asking how can God do this or that we need to tread very softly, for God is a being of infinite wisdom and we know almost nothing. When we think how vast God is and how infinitesimal we are we do well to hesitate about questioning as to how God can do anything. An infinitely wise God may have a thousand good reasons for doing things when we in our almost utter ignorance cannot see one good or even possible reason.

Having said this much we may add that evil seems to be a necessary accompaniment of good. Moral good is the highest good, and freedom of choice is necessary to the attainment of moral good. In fact, no being can be good in the highest sense unless it is possible for him to do evil, but if it is possible for him to do evil he may do it. God created all beings good, but the highest beings were created with the power of choice. They could choose disobedience to God if they would.

53

One of the very highest of such beings, he whom we now call Satan, chose evil. God created man also with the power of choice, and the first man chose evil, and the whole race followed him. Thus evil entered into the world as the outcome of God's having created man on the highest plane, that is, with the lofty power of choice.

God permits evil to continue in the world until He has fully worked out His own beneficient plans. When we come to see no longer through a glass darkly but face to face we will doubtless rejoice that God did permit evil to exist in the world.

FAITH

What do you mean by justification by faith?
Is faith the only means of salvation?

The Greek word rendered "to justify" in the New Testament according to its etymology means "to make righteous," but this meaning is extremely rare in Greek usage, if not altogether doubtful, and it certainly is not the New Testament usage of the word. "To justify" in Biblical usage signifies not "to make righteous" but "to reckon, declare, or show to be righteous." A man is justified before God when God reckons him righteous, that is, when God not only forgives his sins but puts all positive righteousness to his account.

There is one condition upon which men are justified before God: simple faith in Jesus Christ (Romans 3:26; 4:5; 5:1; Acts 13:39). It is the atoning death of Jesus Christ on the cross in our place that secures justification for us (Romans 5:9; Galatians 3:13; II Corinthians 5:21). His shed blood is the ground of our justification, and simple faith in Him makes that shed blood ours. Provision is made for our justification by the shedding of His blood; we are actually justified when we believe in Him who shed His blood. Faith is the only means of appropriating to ourselves the atoning virtue that there is in the blood of Jesus Christ. If one will not believe there is nothing he can do that will bring him justification. If one does believe he is justified from all things the moment he believes (Acts 13:38, 39). Not only are all his sins put out of God's sight, but in God's reckoning all of God's own righteousness in Jesus Christ is put to his account. When Jesus Christ died upon the cross of Calvary, He took our place (Gal. 3:10, 13), and the moment we believe on Him we step into His place, and are just as pleasing to God as Jesus Christ Himself is.

I would like to believe, but cannot. Will God condemn me for something I cannot do?

No, God will not condemn you for something you cannot do; but you can believe. Any one can believe. There is plenty of proof that the Bible is the Word of God and that Jesus Christ is the Son of God, proof enough to convince any one who really wants to know and obey the truth.

The Bible is God's Word and Jesus Christ is God's Son. There is plenty of proof in the Bible itself. John says in John 20:31: "These are written (that is, the things contained in the Gospel of John) that ye might believe that Jesus is the Christ, the Son of God, and that believing ye might have life through His name." We here see that life comes through believing that Jesus is the Christ, the Son of God, and that believing that Jesus is the Christ, the Son of God, comes through studying what is written. If any one will take the Gospel of John and read it the right way he will know and believe before he gets through that Jesus is the Christ, the Son of God, and he will have life through believing it. Now what is the right way to read it?

First of all, surrender your will to God. "If any man willeth to do God's will, he shall know of the teaching that it is from God" (John 7:17, R. V.). One can read the Gospel of John again and again and not come to believe that Jesus is the Christ, the Son of God, if he reads it with an unsurrendered will, but if a man will first surrender his will to God to obey God whatever it may cost him he cannot read the Gospel of John through once without coming to see that Jesus is the Christ, the Son of the living God.

Second, each time you read, look up to God and ask Him to

show you how much of truth there is in the verses you are about to read, and promise Him that you will take your stand upon what He shows you to be true. Do not read too many verses at once. Pay careful attention to what you read. Read with a real desire to learn the truth and to obey it. By the time you get through the Gospel you will find that you can believe. In fact, you will find that you do believe.

The reason that men do not believe is either because they are not living up to what they do believe, they have not surrendered their wills to God, or else they do not study the evidence that is calculated to produce belief. Men neglect their Bibles and read all kinds of trashy unbelieving books and then keep saying:

"I can't believe! I can't believe!"

A man might just as well feed himself on poison instead of food and then complain that he is not healthy. There is abundant evidence that Jesus Christ is the Son of God, and faith is a matter of the will—it is willingness to yield to the sufficient evidence. Unbelief is the refusal to yield to the sufficient evidence. Unbelief is a matter for which every unbeliever is responsible.

God demands that we believe, that we yield our wills to the truth which He has abundantly revealed. Faith is the one thing that God demands of man, because it is the one thing above all else that we owe to God (John 6:29). Without that faith which is due to God it is impossible to please Him (Hebrews 11:6). If I had a child that did not believe in me nothing else that he could do would please me.

FALLING FROM GRACE

How do you harmonize the Calvinistic view of the perseverance of the saints with the Arminian belief of falling from grace?

If I understand the Calvinistic view it does not teach the perseverance of the saints but the perseverance of the Saviour.

While it teaches that the saints are utterly unreliable and might fall away any day or any hour it also teaches that the Saviour is ever watchful and ever faithful—for He ever liveth to make intercession for the believer (Hebrews 7:25)—and that He has pledged Himself that those who believe on Him shall never perish (John 10:28), and has given His word for it that He and His Father will keep us to the end, and that no man is able to snatch us out of His hand or that of the Father (John 10:28, 29, R. V.). This does not mean that if a man is once born again and then lies down in sin he will not be lost forever. It means that Jesus Christ will see to it that the one who is born again will not lie down in sin. He may fall into sin, he may fall into gross sin, but Jesus Christ has undertaken his recovery. He will go after the lost sheep until He find it (Luke 15:4). There is no warrant here for one to continue in sin saying: "I am a child of God and therefore cannot be lost." There is no comfort whatever here for such a one. If one lies down in sin and continues in sin it is a proof that he is not a child of God, is not saved, never was regenerate (I John 2:19).

What the Arminians object to is not the doctrine of the faithfulness of the Saviour, that He will prove true even though we prove faithless; what they object to is such a doctrine of "once in grace, always in grace" as enables a man to go on sinning and seeking to justify himself by saying: "I have been saved, therefore I have been in grace and am in grace still."

We need to be on our guard on the one hand against the doctrine that gives us comfort in continuance in sin. We need to be on our guard on the other hand against that distrust of Jesus Christ that makes us fear that some time we shall prove unfaithful and Jesus Christ will desert us. The position that we ought to hold is that held by the apostle Paul, where he asserts on the one hand: "I know whom I have believed, and am persuaded that He is able to keep that which I have committed unto Him against that day" (II Timothy 1:12), but which leads him on the other hand to keep his body under (to give his body a black eye) lest when he has

57

preached to others he himself should become a castaway (I Corinthians 9:27).

FASTING

Ought Christians to fast?

Yes, Christians ought to do anything in their power that will bring blessing to themselves or others, and beyond a question fasting brings blessing in many instances to the one who fasts and in many instances to others.

It is sometimes said that fasting belonged to the Jewish religion but not to the Christian, but this contradicts the plain teaching of the Bible. In Acts 13:2 we are told that it was while they "ministered to the Lord and *fasted*" that the Holy Ghost spoke to the leaders of the church in Antioch. In the third verse we are told that it was after they had "*fasted* and prayed" that they laid their hands on Saul and Barnabas, and sent them away. In Acts 14:23 we are told that at the ordination of elders they "prayed, with *fasting*." There is no virtue in one's going without his necessary food, but there is power in that sense of our own unworthiness that leads us to humble ourselves before God by fasting, and in that downright earnestness in seeking the face of God that leads one away even from his necessary food that he may give himself up to prayer.

If there were more fasting and prayer and less feasting and frolic in the church of Jesus Christ today we would see more revivals and more wonderful things wrought for God.

A FAULTLESS LIFE

Can a person live a faultless life?

No one does live a faultless life and no one can live a faultless life unless he is perfect in knowledge. The sincerest men and women may make mistakes in moral judgment. We are constantly growing in our knowledge of God's will as we study His Word. If at any point we fall below God's highest will our life is not *faultless*.

But while we cannot live a faultless life we can live a *blameless* life, that is, we can live up to our highest understanding of God's will as revealed in His Word. We are not to blame for what we do not know except when our lack of knowledge is the result of our own neglect. (See Colossians 1:22, I Thessalonians 2:10; 3:13; 5:23; etc.)

Every child of God should aim to lead a blameless life, but those who lead the most blameless lives are the most conscious of their deficiencies and know how far their lives are from being absolutely faultless.

FOOT-WASHING

Why do not Christians generally wash the feet as commanded in John 13:4-16?

There is no commandment here that every Christian should wash every other Christian's feet. Nor is there today any church in which every Christian washes every other Christian's feet. There is a command here that when some other Christian needs to have his feet washed (John 13:10) we should be ready to perform even so menial a service as this for him, and thus do as Jesus did to His disciples in their need.

There is not the slightest indication that Jesus at this time appointed a ceremony to be performed in the church. The disciples came in from the road with their feet dusty. They had already bathed earlier in the day (vv. 9, 10, R. V.), and therefore did not need a total ablution, but with their open sandals their feet had become dusty. Each one of them was too proud to wash the other disciples' feet. There was no servant present to do it, so Jesus, though He knew He had come from the Father and was going to the Father, and that the Father had given all things into His hands, arose from the table and performed for them the menial service that was needed.

This is as unlike as can be imagined from the mere performance of the ceremony of washing feet that do not need to be washed for the sake of doing the same thing that Jesus did. The lesson of the passage is plain enough, namely, that we ought to have that love for one another that makes us ready to perform the lowliest service for one another.

FOREKNOWLEDGE AND FOREORDINATION

How do you reconcile man's freedom of choice with God's foreknowledge and foreordination?

Please explain the meaning of the passage: "Being delivered by the determinate counsel and foreknowledge of God" (Acts 2:23).

This means that the actions of Judas and the rest were taken into God's plan, and thus made a part of it. But it does not mean that these men were not perfectly free in their choice. They did not do as they did because God knew that they would do so, but the fact that they would do so was the basis upon which God knew it. Foreknowledge no more determines a man's actions than after-knowledge. Knowledge is determined by the fact, not the fact by knowledge.

Practically the same explanation applies to Romans 8:29, 30: "Whom He did foreknow He did also predestinate to be conformed to the image of His Son."

Kindly explain Acts 13:48—"And as many as were ordained to eternal life believed." Are some born to be lost?

God knows from all eternity what each man will do, whether he will yield to the Spirit and accept Christ, or whether he will resist the Spirit and refuse Christ. Those who will receive Him are ordained to eternal life. If any are lost it is simply because they will not come to Christ and thus obtain life (John 5:40). Whosoever will may come (Revelation 22:17), and all who do come will be received (John 6:37).

God does not ordain any one to be lost *against his own will*, but in God's infinite wisdom and holiness it is ordained that whosoever deliberately and persistently rejects His glorious Son shall be banished forever from His presence.

FOREIGN MISSIONS

What part ought foreign missions to have in the life of the church and the individual believer?

A very prominent part. Our Lord's last command to His disciples was: "Go ye therefore and make disciples of all the nations" (Matthew 28:19). It was in connection with this work that He promised His own personal fellowship. He said that when we did this: "Lo, I am with you alway, even unto the end of the world." If then the individual believer wishes to have personal fellowship with Jesus Christ he must go into all the world and make disciples of all the nations. He may not be able to go in his own person, but in that case he can go by his gifts and by his prayers. Any Christian who is not deeply interested in foreign missions is not in fellowship with Jesus Christ.

Since a true church is a company of obedient believers, what is true of each believer will be true of the church, with the added power and blessing that issues from co-operation.

FORGIVENESS OF SINS

What does John 20:23 mean: "Whose soever sins ye remit, they are remitted unto them; and whose soever sins ye retain, they are retained"? A Roman Catholic said to me that this passage taught that the priest had power on earth to forgive sins. Does it teach this?

The meaning of the verse is very clear if you notice exactly what is said and the exact connection in which Jesus said it. In the preceding verse Jesus had breathed on the disciples and said to them: "Receive ye the Holy Spirit." Then He said

61

to them: "Whose soever sins ye forgive, they are forgiven unto them; and whose soever sins ye retain, they are retained" (R.V.). In other words, Jesus taught that a disciple who had received the Holy Spirit would get the power of spiritual discernment whereby he would know whether there had been true repentance or not, and whose soever sins this Spirit-filled disciple pronounced forgiven, they were indeed forgiven.

The promise was not made to an official priest but to disciples who had been filled with the Holy Spirit. If a priest were filled with the Holy Spirit he doubtless would receive this spiritual discernment, but a man who is not a priest (except in the sense that all believers are priests) and who receives the Holy Spirit may have this spiritual discernment. There are times when any Spirit-filled man knows that a pretence of repentance which another man makes is not genuine, and because of this he declares to that man that his sins are not forgiven, and that man's sins are not forgiven. On other occasions he will see that repentance and faith are genuine and declare to the man that his sins are forgiven.

Peter, filled with the Holy Spirit, exercised this power in Acts 8:20-23. Paul, filled with the Holy Spirit exercised it in Acts 13:9-11. And many a humble believer has this Spirit-given discernment today. There is no mention whatever of priests in the passage, and absolutely nothing that the Roman Catholic can build upon to prove that the priest as such has power on earth to forgive sins.

THE FUTURE LIFE

What becomes of our spirits when we die?

Does the Bible teach an intermediate state of the dead?

Upon death does one's soul pass straightway to heaven or hell, or is there an intermediate state?

Immediately at death the spirit of the believer departs to be with Christ in a state which is very far better than that in which it exists here on earth (Philippians 1:23, R. V.). It is "absent from the body, at home with the Lord" (II Corinthians 5:6-8, R. V.). But this is not the final state of blessedness of the redeemed. In our final state of blessedness the spirit is not merely unclothed from its present mortal body but clothed upon with its resurrection body (II Corinthians 5:1-4). We obtain this resurrection body at the second coming of Christ, when the bodies of those that sleep in Christ are raised from the dead (I Thessalonians 4:15) and the bodies of believers then living are transformed in the twinkling of an eye and this corruptible puts on incorruption (I Corinthians 15:51-53).

On the other hand, immediately at death the spirits of the wicked depart into that portion of Hades reserved for the wicked dead, where they exist in conscious and great torment (Luke 16:19-31). But this is not their final condition of torment. At the close of the millennium those who have died in sin are raised again to stand before the great white throne of God and to be judged and assigned to their final condition of torment (Revelation 20:11-15; 21:8). It is then that they enter into their final and fullest suffering. Just as the redeemed spirit is clothed upon at the coming of Christ with its glorious resurrection body, perfect counterpart of the redeemed spirit that inhabits it and partaker with it in all its joy, so the wicked are to be clothed upon with a body, perfect counterpart of the lost spirit that inhabits it and partaker with it in all its misery.

GIVING

Do you believe in tithing your income for religious purposes?

Yes, as the starting point in Christian giving.

What is the Bible rule for a Christian in the matter of giving money for religious work?

The Christian is not under law in the matter of giving. That is to say, there is no absolute law laid down that a Christian should give just so much and no more. A Christian should consecrate all that he has to God. Every penny of his money should belong to Him. The money he spends upon himself and his family should be spent that way because he thinks God would be more honored if he spent it that way than some other way.

The Jew was under the law to give one-tenth of his income, and over and above that he was expected to give freewill offerings. This Jewish law ought to be a suggestion to us as to where we should begin our giving. We should begin by giving one-tenth to Christ, for a Christian certainly ought not to be less generous than a Jew. But a Christian should not stop with a tenth. He should seek guidance as to the use of every penny he has in addition to the tenth.

Many who follow the plan of giving one-tenth have found great blessing in it, and many have found a prosperity in their business after they have set apart one-tenth to the Lord that they never found before. Most Christians who do not give a tenth fancy that they give more than a tenth, but when they come to set apart the tenth of their income they find that they have much more to give than they had before.

The "rule of three" given by Paul to the Corinthian church in connection with the collection for the poor Christians in Jerusalem contains helpful principles for giving: "(1) Upon the first day of the week (2) let every one of you lay by him in store (3) as God hath prospered him" (I Corinthians 16:2).

Does Matthew 5:42 teach that a Christian should give to every one who asks him for money if he has it in his pocket?

Matthew 5:42 undoubtedly teaches that the disciple of Jesus Christ should give to everyone that asks of him, but it does not teach that he should necessarily give money. When Peter and John were appealed to in Acts 3:2-4 by the lame man at the Gate Beautiful they gave to him, but they did not give him money—they gave him something better. Paul distinctly says in II Thessalonians 3:10: "If any man will not work, neither let him eat." This does not mean that if a man is a tramp we should not give him when he asks, but it does mean that we should use discrimination in what we give him.

Immediately after the verse in Matthew referred to Jesus tells us to be like our heavenly Father who "maketh His sun to rise on the evil and on the good, and on the just and the unjust." Our giving should be patterned after our Father's. He gives to every one that asks, but He does not always give just what they ask.

GOD

Do the names "God," "Lord," and "Lord God," all mean the same person—God?

Yes, in the Old Testament. They are different names of the deity standing for different conceptions of Him. The name "God" is the more general name of the deity. The name "Lord," printed in small capitals in the Authorized Version and the equivalent of "Jehovah" (see American Standard Bible), is the name of God regarded as the covenant God of Israel. The name "Lord" is generally used of Jesus in the New Testament.

There is a school of critics that would have us think that the use of these different names of the deity indicates a different authorship of the different portions of Scripture where the names are used. This for a long time was the favorite argument of the destructive critics, who tried to make out that the Pentateuch (for example) was a patchwork of portions written by different men, but the argument has been thoroughly discredited.

The names of God are very carefully used in the Bible, and make an interesting and profitable study.

How would you prove the existence of God to an inquirer?

It would depend somewhat upon the inquirer. If he was an earnest seeker after truth I would pursue one line. If he was a mere trifler I would pursue another.

In general, I would ask a man what he did believe. I would ask him specifically:

"Do you believe there is an absolute difference between right and wrong?"

In 999 cases out of 1,000 he would answer: "Yes."

Then I would say to him: "The way to get more light is to live up to the light you have, the way to get more truth is to live up to the truth you have. You say you believe there is an absolute difference between right and wrong: will you live up to that? Will you take your stand upon the right to follow it wherever it carries you?"

Very likely he would try to dodge, but I would hold him right to it. If finally he said: "No," then I would say to him:

"The trouble with you is not in regard to what you do not believe, but in fact that you do not live up to what you do believe."

He would see that and be silenced. If he said that he would take his stand upon the right to follow it wherever it carried him, I would next say:

"Do you know that there is not a God?"

Of course he would answer: "No."

Then: "Do you know that God does not answer prayer?"

Very likely he would answer: "I do not know that He does not answer prayer, but I do not believe He does."

I would answer: "I know that He does, but that will not do you any good, but I will show you how to put this thing to the test. The method of modern science is this, that when you find a possible clue to knowledge you follow it out to see what there is in it. Now here is a possible clue to knowledge. Will you adopt the scientific method and follow it out to see what there is in it? Will you pray this prayer: 'O God, if there be any God, show me if Jesus Christ is Thy Son or not, and if Thou showest me that He is I promise to accept Him as my Saviour and confess Him as such before the world' ? "

Here very likely he would try to dodge again, but I would hold him right to it. If he would not agree to this I would show him he was not an honest seeker after truth. If he agreed to do it I would take him another step. I would turn him to John 20:31: "But these are written that ye might

66

believe that Jesus is the Christ, the Son of God, and that believing ye might have life through His name," then say:

"Now here John presents the evidence that Jesus is the Son of God. Will you take the evidence and read it? Will you read the Gospel of John?"

Very likely he would reply: "I have read it already."

I would answer: "Yes, but I want you to read it a new way, read it slowly and thoughtfully, paying attention to what you read. I do not ask you to believe it, I do not ask you to try to believe it, I simply ask you to read it honestly, willing to believe if it be the truth, and each time before you read to offer this prayer: 'O God, if there be any God, show me what truth there is in these verses I am about to read, and what Thou showest me to be true I promise to take my stand upon.'"

If he refused to do this I would show him he was not an honest seeker after the truth, that his unbelief was not his misfortune but his fault. If he agreed to do it I would go over the three things he had agreed to do and then say to him:

"When you get through the Gospel of John will you report to me the result?"

If you do not do this he is very likely to go away and not do what he has promised. I have never had one report to me that he had actually done the things I asked him to do who did not arrive not only at faith in God but in Jesus Christ as His Son and the Bible as His Word. I have tried it with all kinds and conditions of men.

Sometimes I begin at once with a man to show him that there is a God from the evidence of design in nature.

I take out my watch and say:

"Do you think that watch had an intelligent maker?"

The inquirer replies: "Yes."

I ask: "Why do you think it had an intelligent maker? Did you see the watch made?"

"No."

"Then why do you think it had an intelligent maker?"

He will answer: "The watch shows the marks of intelligent

design, thus proving it had an intelligent maker."

Then I say to him: "What about your own eye? Is it not as wonderful a piece of mechanism as a watch? Did it not then have a Maker?"

Everywhere in nature we find symmetry, order, beauty, law, adaptation of means to end. In the minutest forms of being discernible by the most powerful miscroscope we see the same symmetry, order, beauty, law, adaptation of means to ends that are observable in the larger objects with which we are familiar. All this goes to prove the existence of an intelligent Creator and Designer of the physical universe.

The modern evolutionary hypothesis, even if true, would not take away any of the force of the argument from design in nature, for if it were true that the universe as we see it today with all its countless forms of beauty and utility came into being by a process of development from some primordial protoplasm the question would at once arise: Who put into the primordial protoplasm the power of development into the universe as we see it today?

From nature, then, we learn the existence of an intelligent, powerful and beneficent creator. Of course, nature does not teach us some of the profounder truths about God.

What reasons have we for being sure that there is a personal God?

There are many conclusive proofs of the existence of a personal God.

First of all, there is the proof from the marks of *design in nature,* as referred to in the previous answer.

History also proves the existence of a personal God. While sometimes if we look only at a little patch of history it seems as if there was no intelligent and beneficent purpose in it, if we look at history in a large way, following its course through the centuries, we soon discover that back of the conflicting passions and ambitions of men there is some intelligent and beneficent and righteous power restraining and constraining man, and making the wrath of men to praise Him. We find in history that there is "a power, not ourselves, that makes for righteousness." From history we discover that there is a moral governor of the universe. Everything in the universe is attuned to virtue. Everything in nature and history conspires to punish sin and reward virtue. This is a proof of the existence of a personal God.

But *the history of Jesus of Nazareth,* as recorded in the four Gospels, in an especial way proves the existence of a personal God. It is one of the first principles of science that every effect must have an adequate cause, and the only cause that is adequate to account for the character, conduct and works of Jesus of Nazareth is such a God as the Bible reveals. The attempt has been made over and over again, and is being made still, to discount the miraculous in the history of Jesus of Nazareth—indeed, the attempt is made to eliminate the miracles altogether from that story, but every attempt of that kind has resulted in total failure. The ablest effort of that kind was that made many years ago by David Strauss in his *Leben Jesu,* and for a while it seemed to a great many persons as if David Strauss had succeeded. His theories were almost universally accepted in the universities of Europe. But his book would not bear careful critical examination, and after a while was totally discredited, and today nobody accepts Strauss' interpretation of the life of Jesus. Every other attempt of the same kind has met with similar failure, and today for any candid student of the New Testament this much at least is settled, that the story of Jesus of Nazareth as recorded in the four Gospels is at least substantially accurate history. (To my mind far more than this is proven, but that is enough for our present purpose.) If that be true—and it cannot be honestly denied by anyone who goes into the evidence— then the existence of a personal God is proven. Only a personal God will account for the life, character, conduct, miracles, above all for the resurrection from the dead, of Jesus of Nazareth.

But the supreme proof of the existence of a personal God is found in *the experience of the individual believer in Jesus Christ.* Every real Christian knows God in personal experience. I know God more surely than I know any human being.

I once doubted the existence of a personal God. I did not deny His existence, I simply questioned it. I was not an atheist, I was an agnostic. But I determined if there were a God I would know it. I became convinced from the study of history of the probability of the existence of God, but to me at that time it was only a theory. But I made up my mind to put to the test of rigid, personal experiment the theory that there was a God, and that the God of the Bible was the true God. I risked every thing that men hold dear upon this theory. If there had been no God, or if the God of the Bible had not been the true God, I would have lost years ago everything that men hold dear. But I risked, and I won, and today I know that there is a God, and that the God of the Bible is the true God, and every other person may also know it by doing what I did. There was a time in my life when I was put into a place where I literally lived by prayer to the God of the Bible, in the condition so clearly stated in the Bible. Every penny that came to me for the support of myself and wife and four children, for rent of home and of halls, for missionaries, and for everything else, came in answer to prayer. I took the ground that I would not go in debt a cent for anything, that when I could not pay I would not buy. I gave up my salary, ceased taking collections or offerings, told no one but God of any need. This went on for days, and weeks, and months. Every source of former income was cut off, and yet the money came, sometimes in very ordinary ways, sometimes in apparently most extraordinary ways, but it always came, and when I got through I knew there is a personal God and that the God of the Bible is the true God. To me God is the one great reality who gives reality to all other realities.

What do you mean by saying God is a person? Has God a body, or is He merely an invisible spirit?

When we say that God is a person we do not mean that He is possessed of hands, and feet, and legs, and eyes, and nose. These are marks of corporeity, not of personality. When we say that God is a person we mean that He is a being who knows, and feels, and wills, and is not merely blind, unintelligent force. Jesus says in John 4:24: "God is (a) spirit, and they that worship Him must worship Him in spirit and in truth." And in Colossians 1:15 we read that God is "invisible" or unseeable.

But while God in His eternal essence is unseeable He does manifest Himself in visible form. For example, we read in Exodus 24:9, 10 that Moses and Aaron, Nadab and Abihu, and seventy of the elders saw the God of Israel. It is also clear from a study of the different passages in the Old Testament where "the Angel of the LORD" is mentioned that it was God Himself who manifested Himself in this being. We are taught in Philippians 2:6 that Christ Jesus existed originally (see margin, R. V.) "in the form of God." The Greek word translated "form" in this passage means the outward form, that by which one is visible to the eye, and the thought beyond a question is that Jesus Christ in His original state was seen by the angelic world in a form that was outwardly manifest as divine. We may safely conclude from this and other passages of Scripture that while God in His eternal essence is purely spiritual and invisible, nevertheless He manifests Himself in the angelic world and has manifested Himself from all eternity in an outward, visible form.

What do you mean by the Trinity?
How can God be three persons and at the same time one?

God cannot be one and three at the same time, and in the same sense, and the Bible nowhere teaches that God is one and three in the same sense.

But in what sense can He be one and three?

A perfectly satisfactory answer to this question may be impossible from the very nature of the case. First, because God is spirit, and numbers belong primarily to the physical world. Difficulty must inevitably arise when we attempt to describe the facts of spiritual being in the forms of physical expression. Second, because God is infinite, and we are finite. Our attempts at a philosophical explanation of the tri-unity of God is an attempt to put the facts of infinite being into the forms

71

of finite thought. Such an attempt at the very best can only be partially successful. The doctrine of the Trinity, which has been the accepted doctrine of the church through so many centuries, is the most successful attempt in that direction, but it may be questioned whether it is a full and final statement of the truth.

This much we know, that God is essentially one, and we also know that there are three persons possessed of the attributes of deity—the Father, the Son and the Holy Ghost, who are called God, and who are to be worshiped as God. There is but one God, but this one God makes Himself known to us as Father, Son and Holy Spirit. But the Son and the Spirit are both subordinate to the Father. God the Father is God in the absolute and final sense, God in the source. The Son is God in the outflow, but there is all the perfection of the fountain in the river that flows forth from the fountain, and to the Son the Father has imparted all His own perfections, so that it may be said without qualification that "he that hath seen the Son hath seen the Father" (John 14:9). Through all eternity the Son has existed and has possessed of all the perfections of the Father. While He possesses all the perfections of the Father He is not the Father, but is derived from the Father, and is eternally subordinate to the Father. This seems to be as far as we can go now. How much farther we may go in that glad coming day when we shall no longer see through a glass darkly but face to face (I Corinthians 13:12), when we shall no longer know in part but shall know God as perfectly and as thoroughly as He now knows us, none of us can tell.

If God is a God of mercy and love and the director of the universe, why does He send earthquakes, tidal waves and other phenomena when thousands of lives are lost almost instantly?

Because He sees fit to do so.

If God saw fit He would have a perfect right to plunge the whole earth beneath a flood and leave us all to perish instantly. All men have sinned. All men deserve the wrath of God, but God loves even a sinful and apostate race, and He has provided a way of pardon for all who will accept it, and not only a way of pardon but a way whereby we may become sons of God and heirs of God and joint heirs with Jesus Christ (John 1:12; Romans 8:14-17). Any one who accepts this way of pardon, if he is swept away by an earthquake, tidal wave or other disaster, loses nothing. He departs to be with Christ, which is far better (Philippians 1:23). If any one does not accept this way of pardon he is grossly wicked and ungrateful, and his being swept away by an earthquake, tidal wave or other phenomenon is far less than he deserves and far less than he will receive in the judgment that awaits him in the world to come, not merely for his sins but for the black ingratitude of his trampling under foot the mercy of God so marvelously manifested.

In our day men have largely forgotten that God is God, and they think that He is under obligation to explain His dealings to us.

God's ways are not our ways and God's thoughts are not our thoughts, but as the heavens are higher than the earth, so are His ways higher than our ways and His thoughts than our thoughts (Isaiah 55:8). His judgments are unanswerable and His ways past finding out (Romans 11:33). But when we reach the other side and no longer "see through a glass darkly" but face to face, then we shall understand that the providences of God that were most difficult for us to comprehend in the life that now is were full of mercy and kindness to man. What we all need to learn now is that God in His infinite wisdom may have a thousand good reasons for doing a thing when we in our finite ignorance cannot see even one.

If God exercises general government and control over the entire universe how do you explain the apparent dominance of sin?

It is only on this earth that sin is apparently dominant, and this earth is a very small portion of the universe.

Furthermore, God's plans are eternal and take ages for their full working out. The apparent dominance of sin is only temporary. Through its permission at the present time God is working out His own plans of good. When these plans are wrought out we will see how all the time back of man's failures, rebellions and sin was the controlling power of God. Indeed, we can see it in large measure even at the present time.

GOOD WORKS

May I not merit heaven by my good works?

If your works are absolutely perfect, if you should never break the law of God at any point from the hour of birth until death, if you do all that God requires of you and all that pleases Him, you would merit heaven by your good works.

But this is something that no man but Jesus Christ ever has done. "There is no difference: for all have sinned and come short of the glory of God." (Romans 3:22, 23). The moment that any man breaks the law of God at any point he can no longer merit heaven by his good works. The law demands perfect obedience (Galatians 3:10). Nothing but perfect obedience to the law of God will secure life or heaven. There is, therefore, no hope on the ground of our own works.

The moment a man has sinned at any point his only hope then is that he be justified freely *through the grace of God* in Jesus Christ. But justification by free grace is offered to all who will accept Jesus Christ. All who believe are justified freely (that is, as a free gift) through the redemption that is in Christ Jesus (Romans 3:24). God set Him forth to be the propitiation through faith in His blood (Romans 3:25, R. V.). Study the whole passage Romans 3:9 to 4:8, and you will see how impossible it is that any man can merit heaven by his good works, and what God's method of justification is.

THE HEATHEN

How is God going to judge the heathen?

Can the heathen be saved by following the best light they have?

God will judge the heathen in righteousness, according to the light they have had. Those who have sinned without knowing the law revealed to Moses will also perish without the law, and as many as have sinned under the law shall be judged by the law (Romans 2:12).

The heathen are not without light. The fact that they do by nature the things required in the law shows that they have a law, though not the law revealed to Moses (Romans 2:14). If any heathen should live perfectly up to the light he has he would doubtless be saved by doing so, but no heathen has ever done this. Romans 2:12-16 is often taken as teaching that the heathen are to be saved by the light of nature, but any one who will read the passage carefully in its connection will see that Paul's whole purpose is not to show how the heathen are saved by keeping the law written in their hearts but to show that all are under condemnation—the Jew because he has not lived up to the law given by revelation, and the Gentile because he has not lived up to the law written in his heart. The conclusion of the matter is given in Romans 3:22, 23, R. V.: "For there is no distinction; for *all have sinned* and fall short of the glory of God." In the verses that follow the only way of salvation is pointed out, namely, free justification by God's grace through the redemption that is in Christ Jesus on the ground of His propitiatory death, the value of which each one appropriates to himself by faith in Him. No one will be saved except through personal acceptance of Jesus Christ as his personal Saviour. There is not a line of Scripture that holds out a ray of hope to any one who dies without accepting Jesus Christ.

There are those who hold that those who die without hearing of Jesus Christ in this world will have an opportunity of hearing of Him and accepting Him or rejecting Him in some future state, but the Bible does not say so, and this is pure speculation without a word of Scripture to support it.

There are also those who hold that those heathen who would have accepted Christ if He had been presented to them will be treated as if He had been presented to them and they had accepted Him, but this is all pure speculation.

All the Bible teaches is that no one can be saved without personal acceptance of Christ, and the part of wisdom on our part is to do everything in our power to see the heathen have the opportunity of accepting Christ in the life that now is, for we have not one word of Scripture to support us in the hope that if we neglect our duty here the heathen will have an opportunity to accept Christ in some future age or state.

HEAVEN

Is heaven a place or a state of the soul?

Jesus Christ plainly declares that heaven is a place. In John 14:2 He says: "I go to prepare *a place* for you," and to make it even more plain He adds in the next verse that when the place is prepared He will come again and receive us unto Himself, that *where* He is there we may be also.

Furthermore, we are distinctly told that when Jesus Himself left this earth He went into heaven, from whence He had come (John 13:3; Acts 1:9, 10; Ephesians 1:20, 21; and many other places).

The blessedness of heaven will not all be because of the character of the place. It will be still more because of the state of mind in which those who inhabit heaven will be. Nevertheless, heaven is a place, a place more beautiful than any of us can conceive. All earthly comparisons necessarily fail. In our present state every sense and faculty of perception is blunted by sin and by the disease that results from sin. In our redeemed bodies every sense and faculty will receive enlargement and exist in perfection. There may be new senses, but what they may be we cannot of course now imagine. The fairest sights that we have ever beheld on earth are nothing in beauty to what will greet us in that fair "city that hath foundations." Heaven will be free from everything that curses or mars our lives here. There will be no servile grinding toil, no sickness or pain (Revelation 21:4), no death, no funerals and no separations. Above all, there will be no sin. It will be a place of universal and perfect knowledge (I Corinthians 13:12), of universal and perfect love (I John 3:2; 4:8), of perpetual praise (Revelation 7:9-12). It will be a land of melody and song.

What must one do to get to heaven?

There is just one thing that any one needs to do to get to heaven, that is, to accept Jesus Christ as his personal Saviour, acknowledge Christ as Lord and Master, and openly confess Him as such before the world. Jesus Christ says: "I am the way, the truth and the life. No man cometh unto the Father but by Me" (John 14:6). Again He says: "I am the door. By Me if any man enter in he shall be saved" (John 10:9). Any one who receives Jesus becomes at once a child of God, an heir of God, a joint-heir with Jesus Christ (John 1:12; Romans 8:16, 17).

Any one can know whether he is already on the way to heaven or not by simply asking himself the questions:

"Have I received Jesus Christ? Have I taken Him as my Sin-bearer, the One who bore my sins in His own body on the cross? (Isaiah 53:6; I Peter 2:24; Galatians 3:13.) Am I trusting God to forgive my sins because Jesus Christ bore them for me? Have I taken Jesus Christ as my Lord and Master? Have I surrendered my thoughts to Him to teach and my life to Him to guide in everything? Am I confessing Him as my Saviour and my Lord before the world as I have opportunity?"

If any one can answer yes to these simple questions he may know he is on the way to heaven. Of course, if one has really received Jesus as his Lord and Master he will prove it by studying His Word day by day to know His will, and by doing His will as he finds it revealed in the Bible.

Is the Bible an all-sufficient guide to heaven?

It is. It tells each one of us what sort of a place heaven is and just how to get there. There is not a thing a man needs to know about the road to heaven that is not plainly stated in the Bible. It is the only Book in the world that reveals Jesus Christ, and Jesus Christ is Himself the way to heaven (John 14:6).

Shall we recognize our loved ones in heaven?

Most assuredly we shall. Paul in writing to the believers of Thessalonica tells them not to sorrow over their loved ones, from whom they have been separated for a time, as others who have no hope sorrow over them, for (he goes on to say) Jesus Himself is coming back again, and our loved ones who have fallen asleep in Jesus will be first raised, and then we who are alive will be transformed and caught up *together with them* to meet the Lord in the air. The whole basis of this exhortation is that when we are caught up *together with* our loved ones we shall have them again. Furthermore, Moses and Elijah appeared to the three disciples who were with Christ in the Mount of Transfiguration, and were recognized by them (Matthew 17:3 and following verses). If we shall recognize those whom we have never known in the flesh, how much more shall we recognize our loved ones!

Can a person be happy in heaven if he knows his loved ones are in hell?

Yes, most assuredly, if he is a real Christian. A real Christian's supreme joy is in Jesus Christ (Matthew 10:37). The love that he bears even to the dearest of his earthly loved ones is nothing to that he bears to Jesus Christ, and Jesus Christ is in heaven. He will satisfy every longing of the heart that really knows Him.

Furthermore, if any of our loved ones are in hell they will be there simply because they persistently rejected and trampled under foot that One who is the supreme object of our love. They will be with the Devil and his angels because they chose to cast in their lot with them, and we will recognize the justice of it and the necessity of it. Many will not allow themselves to believe in eternal punishment because they have impenitent friends and loved ones, but it is better far to recognize the facts, no matter how unwelcome they may be, and try to save our loved ones from the doom to which they are certainly hurrying on, than it is to quarrel with facts and seek to remove them by shutting our eyes to them. If we love Jesus Christ supremely, love Him as we would love Him, and realize His glory and His claims upon men as we should realize them, we will say, if the dearest friend we have on earth persists in trampling Christ under foot, he ought to be tormented forever. If after men have sinned and merited God's awful wrath God still offers them mercy and makes the tremendous sacrifice of His Son to save them—if after all this they still despise that mercy, trample God's Son under foot, and are consigned to everlasting torment, any one who sees as he ought to see will say:

"Amen; true and righteous are Thy judgments, O Lord!"

HELL

Is hell a place or state of the soul?

Hell, meaning by this name the final abode of Satan and the impenitent, is plainly declared in the Bible to be a place prepared for the Devil and his angels. The arguments and many Scripture passages are to be found in the answers given under "The Devil" and "Eternal Punishment." See also "Heaven."

Please explain Psalm 139:8: "If I ascend up into heaven Thou are there; if I make my bed in hell, behold, Thou art there!" I cannot conceive of God's presence in hell.

The word rendered "hell" in this passage does not mean hell in the sense of the abode of the lost. It means the place where all the dead were before our Lord's ascension. (It is rendered in the Revised Version—"Sheol." This is not a translation; it is the Hebrew word used.) Both the righteous and unrighteous dead went to Sheol, the righteous to that portion of Sheol known as paradise, and the unrighteous to the place of suffering. But if God is everywhere, He must in some sense be present even in hell, but He certainly does not manifest His presence there as He does in heaven, or even as He does on earth.

THE HOLY SPIRIT

Does the Holy Spirit live in and remain with the believer, or come and go?

I know of no place where it is recorded that He comes and goes from the believer. It is true the Spirit of the Lord departed from king Saul, but we have no reason for believing that he was a true believer, a regenerate man. The Holy Spirit dwells in the believer according to the teaching of Jesus Christ (John 14:17). The believer may grieve Him (Ephesians 4:30), but it does not say that the believer "grieves Him away," as it is sometimes quoted. Indeed, it distinctly says that even though we grieve Him we are "sealed unto the day of redemption." The believer through sin or worldliness may lose the consciousness of the indwelling presence of the Spirit of God, but losing the consciousness of His presence and power is one thing, actually losing His presence is another. The Holy Spirit may withdraw into the innermost sanctuary of the believer's spirit, back of conscious possession, but He is still there.

There is, however, a work of the Holy Spirit upon a person short of regeneration, as in conviction, and in such a case He may come and go.

Please tell something about waiting on God for power for service.

Our Lord Jesus distinctly teaches in Acts 1:8 that there is a definite enduement of power from the Holy Spirit for those who seek it. The experience of thousands of ministers and

80

other believers proves the same. This power is received on the following conditions:

First, that we rest absolutely on the finished work of Christ as the only ground of our acceptance before God. Second, that we put out of our lives every known sin. Third, that we surrender absolutely to God for Him to use us as He will. Fourth, that we openly confess our acceptance of Jesus Christ as our Saviour and Lord before the world. Fifth, that we really desire this anointing. Sixth, that we definitely ask for it. Seventh, that we take by faith what we ask for (Mark 11:24; I John 5:14, 15).

There need be no long time of waiting. God is ready to give the Holy Spirit at once (Luke 11:13). Of course, waiting on God is something that every believer should practice, and doubtless God gives His Spirit when persons individually or together spend a long time in prayer before Him, thus recognizing and acknowledging their dependence upon Him, but the teaching that a man may have to wait a month or six months is wholly without warrant in the Bible.

IMMORTALITY

How do you prove the immortality of the soul?

In the Bible immortality as applied to man is used of the body and not of the soul, but I suppose the question means: How do you prove that there is a future existence after death?

We prove it from the Bible. The Bible teaches beyond a question that all men shall be raised from the dead, the righteous unto the resurrection of life and those that have done evil unto the resurrection of judgment (John 8:28, 29). It furthermore teaches what the exact state of those who accept Christ and of those who reject Christ will be in the future eternal existence. Furthermore the resurrection of Jesus Christ is one of the best proven facts of history, and proves to a demonstration that death does not end all.

There are arguments for immortality of a scientific and philosophical character, but if we leave out those built upon

81

the resurrection of Jesus Christ all that these arguments prove is the probability of life after death, the probability of a future existence; but when we take the Bible in, and above all the resurrection of Jesus Christ, our belief in a future existence is no longer based upon a mere probability, it is removed from the domain of the merely probable into the domain of the absolutely certain and proven.

Do the Scriptures teach conditional immortality?

By the doctrine of conditional immortality is meant the doctrine that man is naturally mortal and only gains immortality in Christ.

There is an element of truth in the doctrine, namely, that man is naturally mortal. As man could begin to be, man could of course cease to be. But it is the plain teaching of Scripture that all the sons of Adam get endless existence in Christ. In I Corinthians 15:22 we are told that "as in Adam all die, even so in Christ shall all be made alive." If we deal fairly with these words, one "all" is as comprehensive as the other. Every one that loses existence in Adam, who returns to the dust (Genesis 3:19; 5:5), is raised from the dust in Christ. The whole race gets back in Christ what it lost in Adam. But whether this existence, this resurrection life, that we get in Christ, shall be a resurrection unto life or a resurrection unto judgment and everlasting shame and contempt (John 5:28, 29; Daniel 12:2) depends entirely upon what we do with the Christ in whom we get it. Every man's endless existence becomes an existence in unspeakable blessedness if he accepts Christ, but that existence becomes an existence in unspeakable misery if he rejects Christ. It is the second death (Revelation 21:8), a part with the Devil and his angels in the lake of fire prepared for them (Matthew 25:41, 46), a portion in the lake of fire where there is no rest day nor night for ever and ever (Revelation 20:10).

INFANTS

Are those who die in infancy lost forever?

There is not a line of Scripture to indicate that they are. Jesus says: "Suffer the little children, and forbid them not to come unto Me, for of such is the kingdom of heaven" (Matthew 19:14, R. V.). It is true that infants are born into this world members of a fallen race under condemnation of God, that Adam's sin is imputed to all his descendants, but the sins of the whole race were atoned for by the death of Jesus Christ on the cross (I Timothy 2:6; John 1:29; I John 2:2). This includes the children.

When a child reaches the age of accountability and sins himself there must needs be a definite personal acceptance of Christ before he can be saved, but of course this does not apply to those who die in infancy. To them Christ's one act of righteousness (His atoning death on the cross) brings the free gift of justification of life (Romans 5:18, R. V.; I Corinthians 15:22). The time will come when these children will see Christ, and believe in Him, and thus be saved in the fullest sense. But they will never perish for Adam's sin. Jesus Christ bore the penalty of Adam's sin for them. No one is lost merely because of Adam's sin. There is absolutely no ground in Scripture for the doctrine of the damnation of unbaptized infants.

Is there any Scripture that goes to show that the children of unbelieving parents will be saved if they die in infancy? If so, what does the latter part of I Corinthians 7:14 mean: "The unbelieving husband is sanctified by the wife, and the unbelieving wife is sanctified by the husband, else were your children unclean; but now are they holy"?

The latter part of this verse undoubtedly teaches that the children of believing parents stand in a different relation to God from the children of unbelieving parents, but there is no teaching in the Bible anywhere that any infant is lost, as explained in the preceding answer.

Where do those who die in their infancy go in the other world?

The Bible does not tell specifically. It does, however, say that "of such is the kingdom of heaven" (Matthew 19:14). There is absolutely no ground in Scripture for the doctrine that while infants do not go to the place of torment they go to a place where there is not that fullness of blessedness which those who live to maturity and accept Jesus Christ enter. We are not wise to go beyond what is written and make theories of our own regarding their future destiny, but certainly there is not the slightest ground for any anxiety regarding them.

INSURANCE

Some people hold that Christians should not insure their lives, property, etc., because by so doing they distrust God and His providential care. What does the Bible teach as to this?

The Bible teaches that there is no conflict between trusting God and an intelligent and wise provision for the necessities of the future, as (for instance) in Proverbs 6:6-8: "Go to the ant, thou sluggard; consider her ways, and be wise; which, having no guide, overseer or ruler, provideth her meat in the summer and gathereth her food in the harvest." When Paul had God's own assurance that both he and all those who were with him on the ship should be saved, and fully believed God that it should come out even as it had been told him, nevertheless when the sailors tried to flee out of the ship and thus imperil the vessel Paul saw to it that they were not allowed to escape (Acts 27:23-25, 30-32). This was not an act of unbelief on Paul's part. It was simply co-operating with God in the fulfillment of God's promise.

Now as to whether it is an intelligent and wise provision for the future to insure one's life or to insure one's property, is another question which each one must decide prayerfully for himself. God promises to each one of us wisdom in the settling of such questions if we look to Him for it and meet the conditions of answered prayer (James 5:1-7). But even if it should prove to be an unnecessary expenditure to insure one's life or property, that would not make it an act of distrust in God.

THE JEWS

Is there any difference today in God's sight between Jews and Gentiles?

Most assuredly there is. In I Corinthians 10:32 the apostle Paul divides men into three classes—the Jews, the Gentiles, and the church of God. God has His plans today for the Jew, His plans for the Gentile, and His plans for the church.

In the church there is neither Jew nor Gentile (Galatians 3:28). When one accepts Jesus Christ as his Saviour, surrenders to Him as his Lord and Master, and openly confesses Him as such before the world, he becomes part of the body of Christ, that is, a part of the church. The relation of the Jewish Christian to Christ is precisely the same as that of the Gentile Christian. The promises that belong to one belong to the other, the Scriptures that belong to one belong to the other.

But outside of the church there is Jew and Gentile, and God's plans are not precisely the same for both. The present dispensation is pre-eminently a Gentile dispensation. The Jew for the time being has been set aside, but his day is coming (Romans 11:25, 26, 30, 31; and many other passages).

The method of dividing the Word that some have, applying some of the promises to Jewish Christians and others to Gentile Christians, is not warranted by the Word. What belongs to any Christian belongs to all Christians, both Jewish and Gentile.

JUDGMENT

Do the Scriptures teach that there will be one general or several judgments?

The Scriptures plainly teach that there will be several judgments. There will be, first of all, the judgment of the believer when he is caught up to meet the Lord in the air, a judgment not regarding his salvation—for that is settled the moment he accepts Christ (John 5:24, R. V.)—but a judgment regarding his reward (I Corinthians 3:13-15; II Timothy 4:8). Then there will be the judgment of the nations living on this earth at the time that the Lord comes with His saints to it, described in Matthew 25:31-46. But those who have not a part in the first resurrection will not be raised for their judgment for a thousand years (Revelation 20:4, 5). At the end of the thousand years, the millennium, the rest of the dead will be raised and appear before God at the judgment of the great white throne (Revelation 20:11-15).

Does God temper the judgment of those who sin ignorantly?

Certainly God does not deal with those who sin ignorantly as He does with those who sin of deliberate and willful choice (see I Timothy 1:13; compare Hebrews 10:26). But there is not a man on this earth who has not sinned knowingly (Romans 3:23), and therefore, there is no hope for any man outside the atoning work of Jesus Christ (Romans 3:24-26). Every one who believes on Jesus Christ receives eternal life, and no one who rejects Him shall see life, but shall perish forever (John 3:36; II Thessalonians 1:7-9).

LAW

**Ought Christians to keep the law of Moses?
Is a Christian under law?**

No. We are taught in Galatians 5:18: "If ye be led by the Spirit ye are not under the law."

But this does not mean for a moment that a Christian is to

lead a lawless life. While we are not under the law of Moses we are under law to Christ (Romans 7:4), that is, we are under obligation to do in all things the things that please our new husband, Christ. Those who are led by the Spirit, who are the only ones who are not under law, will not do things that are forbidden by the Spirit in the Word of God.

There are many in our day who have gone into the most foolish extravagances regarding not being under the law. They say that they are led by the Spirit and therefore are not under any obligation to obey the Word, and they do things which they say the Spirit leads them to do which are directly contrary to the will of God as revealed in the Bible. Now the Bible is the Holy Spirit's book, and the Holy Spirit certainly does not lead one to do things that are contrary to the Bible, and any spirit that leads men to do things that are contrary to the teachings of the Bible is certainly not the Holy Spirit. There are some Christians, for instance, who scoff at all obligation to keep the Lord's Day differently from other days, and ridicule as being under the law those who do set this day apart. These people are unscriptural, and are doing much harm. While they claim to be in subjection to the Holy Spirit they are really in subjection only to their own headstrong self-will and spiritual pride.

THE LORD'S TABLE

Ought we to invite to the Lord's table all who believe themselves to be Christians whether or not they have previously been received into the membership of the church?

Jesus Christ commands all believers: "This do in remembrance of Me" (I Corinthians 11:24); therefore all believers should have the privilege of doing this, whether or not they have previously been received into the membership of the church. But the importance and necessity of church membership should be urged upon all believers.

LOVE FOR SOULS

How may I realize a love for souls?

First, by giving your whole self up, all your thoughts, feelings, ambitions, purposes, to the control of the Holy Spirit. The Holy Spirit loves souls, and if you give yourself up to His control He will impart a love for souls to you. The very first part of the description of the fruit of the Spirit is love (Galatians 5:22).

Second, by dwelling upon the actual condition of men outside of Christ, as revealed in the Word of God, and studying what the Word of God says about their ultimate destiny. If you reflect upon the hell that awaits lost souls you will soon have (if you are a Christian at all) a passion for their salvation.

Third, by observing Jesus Christ and dwelling upon His conduct toward the lost.

MAN IN GOD'S IMAGE

What does Genesis 1:27 mean when it says: "God created man in His own image"?

We are told in Colossians 3:10 that the regenerated man is "renewed *in knowledge* after the image of Him that created him." In Ephesians 4:23, 24 we are told that it is "in righteousness and true holiness" that he is created in the image of God. It is evident then that the words "image" and "likeness" in Genesis 1:26, 27 do not refer to visible or bodily likeness but to intellectual and moral likeness in "knowledge," "righteousness" and "holiness of truth." However, we are taught in Philippians 2:6 (see R. V. margin) that Christ Jesus existed originally "in the form of God," that is, in a visible form that was divine, and in our ultimate state of blessedness we shall be like Christ in our bodily appearance as well as intellectually and morally (I John 3:2; Matthew 17:2; 13:43).

MARRIAGE

Should a Christian ever marry an unbeliever?

Most assuredly not. To do so is to disobey the plainest directions of God's Word. God says in II Corinthians 6:14: "Be not unequally yoked together with unbelievers." When a woman marries a man, or a man a woman, they are yoked together in the most complete and intimate sense. By "unbelievers" in this passage God evidently does not mean merely infidels, but all who have not definitely received Jesus Christ and surrendered their lives to Him.

More promising lives are shipwrecked by a marriage contrary to the Word of God than in almost any other way. Some women marry men for the purpose of converting them. Such marriages result in inevitable and unutterable misery. You cannot hope to convert another by disobeying God yourself.

Do you believe in mixed marriages?

I suppose you mean by "mixed marriages" the marriage of a converted person to an unconverted person. If that is what you mean, the Bible explicitly forbids such marriages in II Corinthians 6:14, quoted in answer to the previous question. Any converted man or any converted woman who marries an unconverted man or an unconverted woman disobeys the plain commandment of God's Word. Doubtless many do this through ignorance, but that does not make it right.

If you mean the marriage of a white person to a Negro or the intermarriage of persons of nationalities widely separated from one another, as (for example) the marriage of a Chinese man to an American or English woman, I do not believe in it. It might be difficult to find Scripture that specifically forbids it, but such a marriage will certainly bring great misery to the resultant offspring, under the present conditions of human society. It brings them into a position almost intolerable, and is therefore a plain violation of our Lord's words: "Whatsoever ye would that men should do, to you, do ye even so to them" (Matthew 7:12). Where a man and woman are separated by wide lines of national demarcation their marriage involves them in difficulties that will hinder, if not absolutely prevent, the largest usefulness for Christ.

If the question refers to marriages between Catholics and Protestants, such a marriage is quite sure to be unfortunate. While Roman Catholics and Protestants may both be real believers in the Lord Jesus Christ the differences between them are so radical that a marriage between the two cannot but result in friction and misunderstanding. Especially will this be true when children are born into the family, and the question of rearing the children comes up. If the two parties in question cannot come to see eye to eye on the essential questions of difference between Catholics and Protestants before their marriage, then they had better not marry.

Is the marriage of cousins sanctioned in the Bible?

There is no explicit commandment in the Bible that cousins should not marry, but it is a well known fact that the marriage of near relatives is fraught with great physical dangers. If there is any hereditary taint in the family it will be accentuated in the children of near relatives. Certainly the Bible does not sanction two persons entering into a marriage, the issue of which is fraught with so great possible peril.

THE USE OF MEDICINE

Does James 5:14,15 ("Is any sick among you? Let him call for the elders of the church, and let them pray over him, anointing him with oil in the name of the Lord; and the prayer of faith shall heal the sick, and the Lord shall raise him up") give ground for believing that medical aid should have no place in the life of faith, or does the Lord expect us to use the means at hand, invoking His blessing upon such means?

This passage does not give ground for believing that medical aid should never have any place in the life of faith. It tells us what we should do when we are sick, but it says nothing either for or against medicine. Doubtless it is oftentimes the purpose of God to heal without any means except those mentioned in this passage, but it is also plainly taught in the Word of God that the use of means may be proper, as in I Timothy 5:23—"Drink no longer water, but use a little wine for thy stomach's sake and thine often infirmities."

THE MILLENNIUM

What is the millennium?

"Millennium" means 1,000 years, and the millennium is the thousand years' reign of Christ on earth after His second coming (Revelation 20:4). There are many prophecies about Christ as an earthly king which are not yet fulfilled but which will be fulfilled in His millennial reign on earth. He will occupy the throne of David (Jeremiah 23:5, 6; Psalm 2:6; Zechariah 14:9). This does not mean that He shall all the time sit on a throne in Jerusalem. The ruler of England occupies the throne of England, but very seldom literally sits upon that throne. It may be that much of the time Christ will be with His bride in the New Jerusalem, and not in the old literal Jerusalem here on earth, but He will reign as king on earth for 1,000 years.

Will the millennium be a period of soul-saving revival?

There seems to be reason to suppose that in connection with the return of our Lord the events that accompany it will result in bringing many persons to their senses and to an acceptance of Jesus Christ. Certainly this is true of Israel. There is to be a national repentance, a national turning to Christ. Jesus, coming as a deliverer, shall turn away ungodliness from Jacob (Romans 11:26). God will pour out upon them the Spirit of grace and of supplications. They shall look upon the One whom they have pierced, and shall mourn over their sin, and a fountain shall be opened to them for sin and for uncleanness, and there shall be a national turning to Jesus Christ (Zechariah 12:10 to 13:1).

In connection with the conversion of Israel there will also be a great turning of the Gentiles to Christ (Romans 11:12).

MIRACLES

How are miracles possible if the laws of nature are fixed?

God is the author of the laws of nature. The laws of nature indicate God's customary ways of working. To what extent they are fixed, it is impossible to say. But even if they were absolutely fixed, that would not make miracles impossible. One of the most universally recognized laws of nature is the law of gravitation. According to the law of gravitation a stone lying on the surface of the earth will be drawn toward the center of the earth, but it is quite possible for a man to come along and if he wills to do so to lift that stone away from the earth. The law of gravitation is not violated in the least, but a higher law, the law of the human will, steps in and produces an effect just the opposite of what the law of gravitation of itself would have produced. If a human being can bring things to pass that the fixed law of nature would not have brought to pass left to itself, how much more can a mighty God who is the Creator of all things!

All this argument about miracles being impossible because of the fixed laws of nature appears wise to the shallow thinker, but when we look right at it it is found to be supremely absurd. The real question is not whether miracles are possible, but rather if they have occurred. Are they well attested. Miracles are certainly well attested. The supreme miracle of all is the resurrection of Jesus Christ from the dead. A leading agnostic has said:

"We need not discuss the other miracles. The whole question is: Did Jesus Christ rise from the dead? If He did it is easy enough to believe the other miracles. If He did not the miraculous must go."

He has well stated the case. If Jesus Christ did rise from the dead then the miraculous is proven. The argument for the resurrection of Jesus Christ from the dead is simply overwhelming. The resurrection of Jesus Christ from the dead is one of the best proven facts of history, so it is plain that miracles are not only possible but historically certain.

Has the age of miracles passed away?
Why doesn't God work miracles today as in Christ's time?

There is no conclusive Bible proof that God does not work miracles today, neither is there any reason in history or experience. That physical miracles should not be so frequent and abundant as they were when Jesus Christ Himself was upon the earth is only to be expected, for then He was God manifest in the flesh, but now He is with us in the spirit, and the miracles that we should expect to see more abundantly in the present time are in the spiritual realm. Regeneration is a miracle. The raising of a spirit dead in trespasses and sins to life in Jesus Christ is a more wonderful miracle than the resurrection of the body. This miracle is being constantly wrought. In fact, those who believe in Jesus Christ today are doing greater things in the spiritual realm than Jesus Christ accomplished while He was here upon earth. This is only the fulfillment of Christ's own word (John 14:12).

We may expect that physical miracles will be more common again when Christ returns the second time, as indicated in many passages in the Bible.

ORIGINAL SIN

What is original sin; how is it just to hold us guilty of it?

The phrase "original sin" is used nowadays in a great variety of senses, and generally inaccurately. Strictly speaking, original sin was the sin in which all other sins originated, that is, the sin of Adam and Eve in the Garden of Eden.

It is just to hold us guilty for this sin—first, because we were all in Adam when he committed the sin; and second, because Adam who was the whole race as it existed at that time sinned as our representative, and we sinned in him (Romans 5:12, R. V.). But when Jesus came as the second Adam He also was our representative, the representative of the whole race, the Son of man, and when He perfectly kept the

93

law of God He kept it as our representative and by His atoning death cleared us from the guilt of the sin committed in Adam (Romans 5:15, 16, 18). No one is lost because of Adam's sin. If any one is lost it will simply be because he does not accept the second Adam.

God's plan of holding us guilty because of Adam's sin is much more merciful than if each of us had had to stand for himself. If each of us had stood for himself we would all have done just what Adam did, we would have sinned, and there would have been no hope; but because the first Adam stood as our representative the second Adam could also stand as our representative, and He did for us what not one of us would have done for ourselves— He perfectly kept the law of God, and having perfectly kept it died for us who had broken it, not only broken it in Adam's sin but broken it in our own personal transgression. There is a depth of mercy as well as wisdom in God's plan that will fill us with wonderment and praise throughout all eternity!

PHYSICAL RESISTANCE

Should a Christian ever make physical resistance when attacked?

I find no warrant in Scripture for his doing so, but a Christian is warranted in defending others when they are attacked by evil men.

PRAYER

How do you know God answers prayer?

I know it first of all *because the Bible says so,* and I have conclusive proof that the Bible is the inerrant Word of God, and whatever it says is true I know to be true. The Bible abounds in statements that God answers prayer. For example, Jesus says in Matthew 7:11: "If ye being evil know how to give good gifts unto your children, how much more shall your Father which is in heaven give good things to

94

them that ask Him!" And He says again to His disciples who were united to Him by a living faith and obedient love: "Whatsoever ye shall ask in My name, that will I do, that the Father may be glorified in the Son. If ye shall ask anything in My name I will do it" (John 14:13, 14).

But I also know that God answers prayer *because He has answered mine*. Time and time again throughout the years I have asked God for things which He alone could give, for things that there was no probability whatever of my getting, and I have told no one else of my need, and God has given me the very things I asked. There have been times in my life when I have asked God for certain specific things, and it was so evident that if I got them they must be from Him that I have said to Him in asking for them: "If you will give me this thing I will never doubt you again as long as I live," and God has given me the very thing I asked. On one occasion God gave $6,000 within two hours in answer to prayer. On another occasion, when another and I prayed for $5,000 for the Moody Bible Institute in Chicago, word was received by telegram that $5,000 had been given for the work by a man who was remote from the place where the prayer was made by about 1,000 miles, and of whose very existence I did not know, who had never given a penny to the Moody Bible Institute before and has never given a penny since. I could multiply instances of this sort.

Now it may be said this is merely coincidence, but the "coincidence" has occurred so often and there has been such an evident connection between prayer (the cause) and the answer (the effect), that to say it is coincidence is to be unscientific.

The history of George Müller's Orphan Homes at Bristol, England, where about 2,000 children have been housed and clothed and fed in answer to prayer through a long period of years, where no money has ever been solicited, no debt ever incurred, and no meal ever failed though oftentimes it seemed as if it might fail up to the very last moment, is to a fair-minded investigator of facts clear proof that God answers prayer. For any one to study the facts in connection with

George Müller's Orphan Homes and still doubt that God answers prayer is for that person not only to be wilfully obstinate in his unbelief but thoroughly unscientific in his treatment of demonstrated facts.

Is not praying asking God to change a law of nature which He established?

It is not. Even an earthly father can answer the prayers of his children without changing the laws of nature. Certainly then the heavenly Father, who made the laws, can answer prayer. God is not the servant of His own laws; His own laws are His servants. If it were necessary to change them in order to answer prayer He could do that, but it is not necessary. For a long time I lived by prayer, everything I had came in answer to prayer. I know God answered my prayers, but I have no reason for supposing that He changed one single law of nature to do it. The laws of nature are not something that govern God, they are simply God's fixed way of acting, fixed by His own free choice.

Why should we tell God our needs when He knows them beforehand?

Because He has told us to do so (Philippians 4:6), and because in this way we are taught what we most need to know—our absolute dependence upon God. There are many things that even an earthly father would give his children if they asked for them, which he would not give them if they did not ask for them. It is for the good of the children that they be required to ask. I for one am very glad that there are some things that God has withheld from me until I ask for them.

To whom may I properly address prayer — to God the Father only?
Is it right to pray to Jesus Christ and to the Holy Spirit?

The normal order of prayer is to the Father, through the Son, in the Spirit (Ephesians 2:18). It is through Christ that we come to God (Hebrews 7:25). God the Father is the ultimate person in prayer.

But there is abundant warrant in the Scriptures for praying to Jesus Christ. In Acts 7:59, R. V., when Stephen was filled with the Spirit we find him calling upon the Lord Jesus. In II Corinthians 12:8, 9 Paul tells us that he besought the Lord thrice for a certain thing, and the context shows that the Lord he besought was Christ. In II Timothy 2:22 Christians are spoken of as "them that call on the Lord," and 4:8 of the same epistle shows the Lord who is meant is the Lord Jesus. In I Corinthians 1:2 Christians are described as those that "call upon the name of Jesus Christ our Lord." In Romans 10:12, 13 we are told that the same Lord over all is rich unto all that "call upon Him," and in v. 9 we are told that the Lord of whom Paul is speaking is the Lord Jesus.

There is only one recorded prayer in the Bible that is addressed to the Holy Spirit (Ezekiel 37:9), but the communion of the Holy Spirit is spoken of (II Corinthians 13:14). Furthermore, Jesus taught that after His departure another Comforter would come to take His place, and that this other Comforter is the Holy Spirit (John 14:16, 17; 15:26). We are dependent upon the Holy Spirit for everything, so must look to Him, which implies prayer. Yet it is the Father and the Son who give the Holy Spirit (John 15:26; Acts 2:33), and it would seem that if we wish Him, instead of praying directly to Him we should pray to the Father or Son for Him.

Why are not all our prayers answered?

For various reasons. Some of our prayers are not answered because we ourselves are not right with God and in a position where God can wisely answer prayer.

Some of them are not answered because they are not offered in the name of Jesus Christ, that is, in dependence upon His claims upon God and not in dependence upon our own. We have no claims upon God. If we approach Him on the ground of our own merit we will get nothing.

Some of our prayers are not answered because they are

not wise, and therefore are not in accordance with the will of God (I John 5:14, 15).

Some of our prayers are not answered because we do not persist in prayer (Luke 11:5-10; 18:1-8).

James says (4:2, 3): "Ye have not because ye ask not. Ye ask, and receive not because ye ask amiss."

If the Lord did not answer your prayers, what would you think was the matter? Would you think it was yourself?

Most assuredly I would. I would go alone with God and ask Him to search me by His Spirit and His Word. If He brought anything to light that was displeasing to Him I would confess it as a sin and put it away. If He did not bring anything to light I would go right along praying, for I have learned that God does not always give us the best things the first time we ask for them, but that He tries and develops our faith and teaches us persistence by keeping us waiting. The longer I live the more I feel that the teaching of Luke 18:1 ("Men ought always to pray, and not to faint") is of the highest importance, and should sink deeply into our hearts.

There was a time when God did not answer my prayers. I was living by faith. Everything I got came in answer to prayer, but the supplies stopped. I cried to God but got no answer. Then I looked up to God and asked Him to search my heart and bring to light anything in my life that displeased Him. He brought to light something that had often troubled me before, but which I would not admit was sin. That night I said: "O God, if this is wrong I will give it up"; but I got no answer. In the bottom of my heart I knew it was wrong all the time. Then I said: "O God, this is wrong, it is sin, I will give it up," and the answer came. The fault was in me, not in God. There is nothing that God more delights to do than to answer prayer.

How shall I pray so as to get what I ask for?

First of all, you must be such a person as the Bible

98

describes as the one whose prayers God answers, that is to say, a person who believes in the Lord Jesus Christ with a living faith and shows the reality of his faith by living a life of daily obedience to His will (John 14:13-15; 15:7; I John 3:22).

Second, you must pray to the Father, through the Son, in the Spirit (Ephesians 2:18). Much that is called prayer is not really prayer to God. There is no thought of God in the mind, no real approach to God in the heart. It is only on the ground of the shed blood of Jesus Christ that one can really approach God and be sure that his prayers are heard (Hebrews 10:19, 20). It is only when we pray in the Holy Spirit, that is, under His guidance, that we pray so we may be sure that God will hear (Jude 20; Romans 8:26, 27).

Third, you must pray according to the will of God (I John 5:14, 15). We may know the will of God by the study of the Word, which is given to us to reveal God's will, and by the leading of the Spirit. Whenever you ask for anything that is promised in the Word of God you may know it is the will of God to give it, and He will give what you ask.

Fourth, one must pray persistently (Luke 11:5-10; 18: 1-8). Here is where many fail. They do not *pray through*. They pray for a thing once or twice, and then conclude it is not God's will to give it. God demands of us that persistent faith that will not take no for an answer. Many a person prays and prays up to the very point of getting a thing, and then fails because he does not pray through.

PROBATION AFTER DEATH

Does Luke 15:4 give clear warrant that Christ is going to continue to seek and to save after death the lost who have had a good opportunity here to repent and come to Christ?

It certainly does not. All that is taught is that the shepherd goes after the lost sheep until he finds it; but not all men are "sheep." The whole argument to prove that this verse teaches that all men will ultimately be found and saved proceeds upon the supposition that all men are *sheep.* But we are distinctly taught in the Word of God that this is not the case. There are sheep and there are goats (Matthew 25:31, 32). There are sheep and there are swine and dogs (II Peter 2:22). Doubtless Jesus Christ will find every one of *His sheep* sooner or later. The Bible teaches that He will find them in the life that now is. But the Bible also teaches that some men are goats and will remain goats up to the judgment day, and to the goats will be said: "Depart from Me, ye cursed, into the eternal fire which is prepared for the devil and his angels" (Matthew 25:41). These are the words of Jesus Himself.

Does not I Peter 3:18, 19 teach another probation after death?

It does teach that Christ, when He was put to death in the flesh (i. e., in His body), was quickened in His spirit, and in His spirit went and preached to the spirits in prison. But we are not told that "the spirits in prison" were men who had lived on the earth and died in their sin. There is reason for supposing that they were the angels who were disobedient in the time of Noah (see v. 20; Genesis 6:1, 2; Jude 6, 7; II Peter 2:4). But even supposing that they were the departed spirits of men who had died in sin we are not told that Jesus preached *the Gospel* to them. The word translated "preach" in this passage does not mean to preach the Gospel, but to herald. There is another word often used in the New Testament which means to preach the Gospel, and it is significant that this word is not used in this passage. Nor are we told that any of these "spirits in prison" to whom Christ preached repented, or even could repent. The passage simply teaches that the kingdom has been heralded in hell as well as in heaven.

Is there any word of Scripture that warrants us to believe in a probation after death?

There is not.

PROSPERITY OF THE WICKED

How is it that a holy and just God allows the wicked to prosper while the good often suffer poverty?

What we call prosperity is often in reality a curse. On the other hand, poverty is often a great blessing. God allows the good to suffer poverty because that is what they most need, all things taken into consideration. One of the things that I often thank God for is that the large amount of money that I expected to inherit from my father never came to me, and that at one time I was allowed to suffer extreme poverty. I have known what it means to be in a foreign land with wife and child, in a strange city where they spoke a strange tongue, and money all gone. I now thank God for it. It may have seemed hard at the time, but it brought great blessing. Poverty drives men nearer to God, makes them feel more deeply their dependence upon Him. It is not something to be dreaded, but something to thank God for.

The psalmist was confronted with this same perplexity. He says in Psalm 73:3: "I was envious at the foolish, when I saw the prosperity of the wicked," and in the 12th and 13th verses he adds: "Behold, these are the ungodly, who prosper in the world; they increase in riches. Verily I have cleansed my heart in vain, and washed my hands in innocency." But further down in the psalm he tells us that all his perplexity was solved when we went into the sanctuary of God, when he communed with God. The mystery was then explained to him, he understood the end of the wicked, he saw how their prosperity was but for a moment, and how God had set them in slippery places, and how they were brought to desolation in a moment. On the other hand, he discovered of himself and of the righteous in general, that even in their poverty they were continually with God, and that God upheld by His right hand; that down in this world of testing and of trial He guides us with His counsel, and that when we come out of the fire purified He afterward receives us into His glory (Psalm 73:24).

Much of our difficulty comes from the fact that we forget

that this world is not all, that this brief world is simply a preparation for a future eternal world, and that happy is the man who has his evil things in this life but in the eternal life to come his good things, and wretched indeed is the man who has his good things in this life and his evil things in that eternal world that is to come (Luke 16:25).

PURGATORY

Is the doctrine of purgatory Scriptural?

The Scriptures do teach an intermediate state after death, but this is not purgatory. See under "Future Life" and "Probation after Death."

RELIGION

What difference does it make what religion a man professes provided he does the best he can?

It makes all the difference in the world. Christianity is true; other religions are false, though they may have elements of truth in them. It does not make a lie any less a lie to believe it most sincerely. Indeed, the more sincerely and heartily a man believes a lie the worse he is off. I may believe that poison is food, and believe it very sincerely, but it will kill me if I take it just as quickly even though I believe it is food as it would had I known it to be poison. If I get on the wrong train, the train going the wrong way, it will not take me to my desired destination no matter how sincerely and earnestly I believe it is going to that destination. It is the truth that sets men free when they believe it, and no amount of earnestness of faith in an error will set me free. Indeed, the more earnestly one believes error the more it will enslave him.

There is no more foolish thought in the world today than that it does not make any difference what a man believes if he is only sincere. What a man really believes determines what a man is, and if he believes error he will be wrong, not only for the life that is to come but for the life that now is, no matter how seriously or earnestly he believes it.

RESURRECTION OF THE BODY

How is it possible we shall rise again with the same bodies we had upon earth?

It is not possible. The Bible does not teach we shall rise again with the same body we had upon earth. It distinctly teaches we shall not rise with the same body. In I Corinthians 15:37, 38 we are told distinctly: "That which thou sowest, thou sowest not that body that shall be, but bare grain, it may chance of wheat or of some other grain; but God giveth it a body as it hath pleased Him, and to every seed his own body." In verse 42 we read: "So also is the resurrection of the dead." That is, as the context clearly shows, just as in our own sowing it is another body that rises, so also in the resurrection of the dead. The body that rises is not the very body that was buried, though it is the outcome of that body. The Bible distinctly teaches that there shall be a resurrection of the body, but not the same body (that is, not composed of exactly the same material elements) that was laid in the grave, but nevertheless a body, a real body. The bodies we now have are sown in corruption, but shall be raised in incorruption. They are sown in dishonor, but shall be raised in glory. They are sown in weakness but shall be raised in power. They are sown a natural body, but shall be raised a spiritual body. There is a natural body, and there is a spiritual body (I Corinthians 15:42-44).

What kind of body shall we have in the resurrection?

It will not be flesh and blood (I Corinthians 15:50, 51), but on the other hand it will not be pure spirit, but have flesh and bones (Luke 24:39). It will be incorruptible—not subject to decay, imperishable, glorious, powerful (I Corinthians 15:42, 43). The days of weariness and weakness will be forever at an end. The body will be able to accomplish all the spirit's purpose. It will be luminous, shining, dazzling, bright like the sun (Matthew 13:43; Daniel 12:3; compare Matthew 17:2; Luke 9:29). Resurrection bodies will differ from one another (I Corinthians 15:41, 42). The resurrection body will

103

be the consummation of our adoption, our placing as sons (Romans 8:23). In the resurrection body it will be outwardly manifest that we are sons of God. Before His incarnation Christ was "in the form of God" (Philippians 2:6), that is, in the visible appearance of God. The word translated "form" in this passage means that with which anything strikes the outward vision. So shall we, in the resurrection, be in the visible appearance of God (compare Colossians 3:4, R. V.; I John 3:2, R. V.).

REWARDS

Is it Scriptural for a Christian to work for reward?

It certainly is. The Bible, constantly holds out rewards, both temporal and eternal, for faithful service. Our Lord Jesus Himself tells us to lay up treasures in heaven (Matthew 6:19-21). The Christian should not serve merely for the reward but out of love to Jesus Christ, but he has a right to expect a reward, and the reward is a great incentive to faithful service.

ROMAN CATHOLICISM

What does Matthew 16:18 mean: "Thou are Peter, and upon this rock I will build My church"? Does this verse teach that Peter was the rock upon which Christ would build His church, and does it prove that the Roman Catholic church as built upon Peter is the only true church?

The passage does not teach that Peter is the rock upon which Christ would build His church. Peter's name in Greek is *Petros*, meaning a piece of rock. The word translated "rock" in the verse is *petra*, which mean a rock.

Peter had just made a confession of Jesus as the Christ, the Son of the living God (v. 16). Jesus, as the Christ, the Son of the living God, is the Rock upon which the church is built. Other foundation can no man lay that this (I Corinthians 3:11). Peter by his faith in Jesus as the Christ, the Son of God, and by his confession of Him as such, became

104

a piece of the Rock. Every believer by believing in Jesus as the Christ, the Son of the living God, and by confessing Him as such, becomes a piece of the Rock, and in that sense a part of the foundation upon which the church is built, Jesus Christ Himself being the chief corner stone (Ephesians 2:20-22).

I cannot believe that the Roman Catholic church is built upon Peter. There is no real evidence that Peter was the first bishop of the church of Rome, and even if he were that would not prove that those who followed him in the office were his true successors. The true successors of Peter are those who build on the same Christ that Peter built upon, who teach the same doctrine and who exhibit the same life.

What does Matthew 16:19 mean: "I will give unto thee the keys of the kingdom of heaven, and whatsoever thou shalt bind on earth shall be bound in heaven, and whatsoever thou shalt loose on earth shall be loosed in heaven"? Does this teach that Peter had the power to admit any one to the kingdom of heaven or shut him out, and that therefore the Roman Catholic church built on Peter is the true church?

No, it does not teach anything of the kind.

When any one studied under a Jewish rabbi it was the custom of the rabbi to give him a key when he had become perfect in the doctrine, signifying that he was now able to unlock the secrets of the kingdom. Christ's words refer to this custom. Peter by the confession of Jesus as the Christ, the Son of God, had proven that the Father was revealing the truth unto him (v. 17), and Jesus looked forward to that day when, filled with the Holy Spirit, Peter would be guided into all the truth (John 16:12-14) and thus be competent to unlock the kingdom to men. Every Spirit-filled man, every one taught by the Holy Spirit, has the keys of the kingdom of heaven. It is my opinion he has spiritual discernment, and is competent to unlock the kingdom to men.

"Binding" and "loosing" were common expressions in Jesus' day for forbidding and permitting. What a rabbi forbade he was said to "bind," what he permitted he was said to "loose."

Peter and the other disciples, as Spirit-filled men, would have discernment to know what God permitted and what God forbade. And whatsoever Peter as a Spirit-filled man forbade on earth would be forbidden in heaven, and whatsoever he permitted would be permitted in heaven.

We see Peter on the day of Pentecost using the keys to unlock the kingdom to the Jews, and 3,000 entered in that day. In the 10th chapter of the Acts we see Peter now using the keys to unlock the kingdom to the Gentiles, and a whole household entered into the kingdom that day.

Every time any man preaches the Gospel in the power of the Holy Spirit he is using the keys. Not only did Peter have the keys, but we may have them today, and being taught by the Spirit we may have discernment as to what God permits and as to what God forbids, and then what we forbid here on earth will be the thing that God in heaven forbids and what we permit will be the thing that God in heaven permits.

Was Peter the first pope?

He was not. There was no pope until long after Peter was dead and buried. The papacy was a later growth, of which there was not even an apparent germ in the days of Peter. So far was Peter from being a pope that the apostle Paul rebuked him openly before them all (Galatians 2:14).

There is no proof that Peter was ever bishop of the church in Rome. There is no decisive proof that he was ever in Rome, but even if he was he certainly was not a pope in any such sense as the word now bears. There is nothing in the Bible that warrants such an office as that of pope. In fact, Jesus Christ expressly forbids any man holding such an office. He says in Matthew 23:8 and following verses: "Be not ye called rabbi, for One is your teacher, even Christ, and all ye are brethren; and call no man your father on the earth, for One is your Father, which is in heaven; neither be ye called masters, for One is your Master, even Christ." Now the pope claims to be a "father" in the very sense used here, in the very sense that Jesus forbids that any man be called father.

THE SABBATH

Why was the Jewish sabbath, or the seventh day of the week which God commanded in the Fourth Commandment to be observed as the sabbath day, changed to the first day of the week, or what we call the Lord's Day, and now observed as the Christian sabbath?

In answer, let me say first of all that there is no commandment in the Ten Commandments which says they were to keep the seventh day *of the week*. The words "of the week" are added by man to the commandment as given by God. What God really commanded through Moses was: "Six days shalt thou labor and do all thy work, but the seventh day is the sabbath of the Lord thy God." It does not say "the seventh day *of the week*"; it says the seventh day after six days of labor. Whether it should be the seventh day of the week or the first day of the week depends upon whether one is a Jew or a Christian. Whether we keep the seventh day of the week or the first day of the week we are keeping the Fourth Commandment to the very letter. If one is a Jew belonging to the old creation let him keep the seventh day of the week, but if he is a Christian and on resurrection ground let him keep the first day of the week, resurrection day.

The Jewish sabbath was not changed to the Lord's Day. The Lord's Day and the Jewish sabbath, while both are a literal keeping of the Fourth Commandment, are not the same day, and do not stand for the same thought. One belongs to the old creation, the other to the new. It is sometimes said by Seventh Day Adventists that there is no authority for the change, and that the Roman Catholic church or the pope made the change. This statement is absolutely untrue. History proves that Christians kept the first day of the week long before there was any Roman Catholic church. We have indications of their keeping it in New Testament times. It was on the first day of the week that the early disciples came together to break bread (Acts 20:7). It was on the first day of the week that believers laid by in store (I Corinthians 16:2), and in the writings of the early fathers, long before the Roman

Catholic church had developed and of course long before there was any pope, we find it stated again and again that the first day of the week was the one that Christians observed.

Paul explicitly teaches that a Christian should not allow himself to be judged in regard to the Jewish sabbath, that the Jewish sabbath belongs along with other Jewish observances in regard to meat and drink, holy days, and new moons, which were the shadow of things to come, but the body is of Christ (Colossians 2:16, 17).

SANCTIFICATION

Some teach that a believer is sanctified instantaneously, others declare that sanctification is a gradual process, perfected in heaven only. What does the Bible teach as to this?

The Bible teaches that every believer is sanctified instantly, the moment he believes on Jesus Christ (I Corinthians 1:2, R. V.; 6:11). The moment any one becomes a member of the church of God by faith in Christ Jesus, that moment he is sanctified. By the offering of the body of Jesus Christ once for all we are cleansed forever from all the guilt of sin. We are "perfected forever" as far as our standing before God is concerned (Hebrews 10:10, 14). The sacrifice does not need to be repeated as the Jewish sacrifices were. The work is done once for all. Sin is put away forever (Hebrews 9:26, compare Galatians 3:13), and we are *set apart* (sanctified) forever as God's peculiar and eternal possession. In this sense every believer is instantly sanctified the moment he believes on Jesus.

But there is still another sense in which every believer may be instantly sanctified. It is his privilege and his duty to present his whole body a living sacrifice to God (Romans 12:1). Such an offering is well-pleasing to God, and when it is made God sends down the fire of the Holy Ghost and takes to Himself what is thus presented. Then instantly the believer so far as his will is concerned is wholly God's or perfectly sanctified.

But after he is perfectly sanctified in this sense, he may

and doubtless often will discover, as he studies the Word of God and as he is taught by the Holy Spirit, that there are individual acts and habits of his life, that there are forms of feeling, speech and action, that are not in conformity with this central purpose of his life. These should be confessed to God as blameworthy and put away, and thus this department of his life also brought by the Holy Spirit into conformity with the will of God as revealed in His Word. But the victory in this newly discovered and unclaimed territory may also be instantaneous. There is no need of a protracted battle. For example, if I should discover in myself an irritability of temper that was manifestly displeasing to God I could go to God at once and confess it and renounce it, and in an instant, not by my own strength but by looking to Jesus and by surrendering this department of my life to the control of the Holy Spirit, overcome it and never have another failure in that direction.

But while there is this instantaneous sanctification that any child of God may claim at any moment, there is also a progressive work of sanctification, an increasing in love, an abounding more and more in a godly walk and in pleasing God, a growing in the grace and knowledge of our Lord and Saviour Jesus Christ, a being transformed into the image of our Lord Jesus Christ from glory unto glory, each new gaze at Him making us more like Him, a growing up into Christ in all things until we attain unto a full grown man, unto the measure of the stature of the fullness of Christ (I Thessalonians 3:12; 4:1, 10. R. V.; II Peter 3:18, R. V.; II Corinthians 3:18, R. V.; Ephesians 4:11-15).

Sanctification becomes complete in the fullest sense at the coming of our Lord and Saviour Jesus Christ (I Thessalonians 5:23, R. V.; 3:12, 13). It is not in the life that now is, nor is it at death, but at the coming of Christ that we are entirely sanctified in this sense.

SECRET ORDERS

Do you believe in secret orders? Do you think it wise to publicly expose them in your preaching?

I do not believe in secret orders, and believe it is wise to show young Christians the peril of them. It ought to be done wisely; I do not believe in making a hobby of that sort of thing. Among the greatest hindrances to the church of Jesus Christ are the masonic and other secret orders. The country churches are filled with women because the lodges have taken the place of the church with men—and even the women are joining their orders. Nevertheless, the first thing I would do would not be to pitch into the lodge; it would be to get men and women converted to Jesus Christ.

Ought a Christian to retain membership in a secret society?

No. I do not see how a Christian who intelligently studies his Bible can do so. The Bible tells us plainly: "Be not unequally yoked together with unbelievers, for what fellowship hath righteousness with unrighteousness, or what fellowship hath light with darkness?" (II Corinthians 6:14). All secret societies of which I have any knowledge are made up, partly at least, of unbelievers, that is, of those who have not accepted Jesus Christ and surrendered their wills to God. In the light of this express commandment of God's Word I do not see how a Christian can retain membership in them. I am not saying that no members of secret societies are Christians, for I have known a great many excellent Christians who were members of secret societies, but how they can continue to be so I cannot see. Many continue members of the masonic and similar orders simply because they are not acquainted with the teachings of the Word of God.

Furthermore, in some secret societies the Scriptures themselves are garbled in the ritual. The name of Jesus Christ is cut out of passages in which it occurs in the Bible so as not to offend non-Christians. How a Christian can retain membership in a society that thus handles deceitfully the Word of

God, and above all cuts out the name of his Lord and Master, I cannot understand.

Further yet, oaths of the most shocking character are required in some secret societies, and there are ceremonies which are simply a caricature of Bible truths, for example there is even a mock resurrection scene.

Further still, Christianity courts the light and not the darkness (Ephesians 5:8, 11, 12). Doubtless many Christians go into the masonic and other orders for the purpose of getting hold of the non-Christian members and winning them for Christ, but this is a mistaken policy. Experience proves that the secret society is more likely to swamp the spiritual life of the Christian than the Christian is to win these members.

SINLESS PERFECTION

Is the doctrine of sinless perfection Scriptural?

How can I John 3: 6, 9 and kindred passages in that epistle be adequately reconciled with I John 1:8, 10?

They can be adequately reconciled by noticing exactly what John says.

In I John 3:6 he says: "Whosoever abideth in Him (that is, in Christ) sinneth not," literally, "is not sinning," that is, is not practicing sin. The verb is in the present tense, which denotes continuous present action. John does not say that he never sins but that he is not making a practice of sin, does not continue sinning, (this being the exact force of the language used).

The same thing may be said of I John 3:9, the literal translation of the opening words of which verse is: "Every one begotten out of God is not doing sin (that is, sin is not his practice), because His seed (that is, God's seed) abideth in him, and he cannot be sinning (be making a practice of sin) because he is begotten out of God."

We should also bear in mind John's definition of sin in the 4th verse of the same chapter: "Sin is lawlessness." In John's usage here sin is the conscious doing of that which is known to be contrary to the will of God. Of course, one who is begotten of God may do that which is contrary to the will of God but which he does not *know* to be contrary to the will of God, and therefore he does not sin in the strict sense in which "sin" is used here. Afterward, when he comes to know the will of God, he will see that it is wrong, and confess and forsake it, but any one begotten of God will not be making a practice of doing that which is known to be contrary to the will of God.

It is plain that there is no contradiction between what is actually said here and between what John actually says in I John 1:8, 10.

In the first of these verses he says: "If we say we have no sin we deceive ourselves." This does not mean that any one who says he is not sinning at the present moment, that he is not doing that which he knows at the present moment to be contrary to the will of God, deceives himself; for there are certainly moments when we can say that we are not at that moment doing that which we know to be contrary to the will of God. But what John says is that if a man says he has no sins to be forgiven, to be cleansed by the blood of Jesus (see context), that is, that he has never sinned, he deceives himself, and the truth is not in him.

In the 10th verse John adds the further thought: "If we say that we have not sinned," we not only deceive ourselves but "we make God a liar, and His word is not in us." A man may not be sinning at the present moment—and if a man is born of God he will not be sinning at the present moment—but nevertheless he has sinned in the past, and if he says he has not he makes God a liar, and His word is not in him. The reconciliation here, as in every other apparent contradiction in the Bible, is found by taking exactly what the inspired authors say.

SPIRITUALISM

Can a Christian be a spiritualist?

An intelligent Christian cannot be a spiritualist, for spiritualism is exposed and condemned in the most unmistakable terms in the Bible.

Spiritualism is not something modern. It is as old as the days of Moses. The mediums in those days had, or professed to have, familiar spirits who spoke through them. Consulting those who had familiar spirits was condemned by God through Moses in the strongest terms. He says (for example) in Leviticus 19:31: "Regard not them that have familiar spirits, neither seek after wizards, to be defiled by them: I am the Lord your God." Again He says in Leviticus 20:6: "And the soul that turneth after such as have familiar spirits, and after wizards, to go a whoring after them, I will even set My face against that soul, and will cut him off from among his people." Again, in Deuteronomy 18:10, 12: "There shall not be found among you any one that maketh his son or his daughter to pass through the fire, or that useth divination, or an observer of times, or an enchanter, or a witch, or a charmer, or a consulter with familiar spirits, or a wizard, or a necromancer. For all that do these things are an abomination unto the Lord: and because of these abominations the Lord thy God doth drive them (the Canaanites) out from before thee." One of the strongest charges brought against Manasseh king of Judah was that he was a spiritualist, and thus provoked God to anger (II Kings 21:1, 2, 6). Saul lost his kingdom and his head for consulting a medium. We read in I Chronicles 10:13, 14: "So Saul died for his transgression which he committed against the Lord, even against the word of the Lord, which he kept not, and also for asking counsel of one that had a familiar spirit, to inquire of it; and inquired not of the Lord: therefore He slew him, and turned the kingdom unto David the son of Jesse."

Nearly all so-called modern spiritualism is a fraud. The tricks of the mediums have been exposed time and time again, but probably it is not all fraud. After all has been explained that can be explained by sleight of hand and natural causes there is still a remnant that points to supernatural origin in some of the manifestations of modern spiritualism. But because it is supernatural it does not prove that it is right or true. According to the teaching of the Bible there is a real unseen world, a world of spirits, but some of the spirits are bad, emissaries and agents of the Devil (Ephesians 6:12; II Thessalonians 2:9-12). The fact that a man or woman can do things and make revelations that we cannot explain by natural causes, things and revelations that seem to show they are peculiarly in contact with the supernatural world, does not prove that they are in league with God. It may rather prove that they are in league with the Devil. It may be that spirits do manifest themselves, but it does not follow that they are the spirits of our departed friends, or other good and wise people who have left this world. There is good reason for believing that these spirits who come to us pretending to be the spirits of our loved ones who have departed, are demoniacal spirits. A prominent medium, who was at that time operating in Chicago, once came to me and said:

"Mr. Torrey, these things are not all sleight of hand and trickery. There are spirits, but they are demons. I was tormented all last night by the demons through whom I do my work."

I asked him why he did not renounce the whole business. He replied that he was making a splendid living through it, and knew of no other way in which he could do so well.

A friend of mine who dabbled in spiritualism and developed unusual powers as a medium was afterward led to renounce the whole business. He went into it thinking it was all right, but he had not gone far before he found it was demoniacal. Many instances of the same thing have occurred.

Even if the spirits manifested are the spirits of our departed loved ones, we are commanded in the Bible not to seek knowledge in this way (Isaiah 8:19, 20), and whoever dabbles in spiritualism at all enters the Devil's territory and disobeys the most explicit commandments of God.

The spiritual and moral influence of spiritualism is ruinous.

114

Sooner or later it leads to the renouncing of Jesus Christ, and to all kinds of free love and other immorality. When we lose our loved ones the temptation often becomes strong to seek communication with them, and thus well-meaning people are led into spiritualism, but it is a snare of the Devil and leads to the eternal ruin of the soul.

TEMPERANCE

What place do you give temperance in your meetings?

A very prominent place. One of the commonest and most destructive sins of our time is that of intemperance. It is doing more to break hearts and ruin homes than almost any other sin, so I constantly attack in my sermons the use of intoxicating liquors, and their sale. I urge upon Christians the duty of total abstinance for their own sake and for the sake of others. I make it a point that if a man can do without intoxicating liquors as well as not, then he ought to do without them for the sake of his brother, but that if he cannot do without them just as well as not he ought to do without them for his own sake.

I do not hold temperance meetings as such. I find it is better to handle the matter as it is handled in the Bible, bringing it in in its proper relation to other things. I never give the pledge to an unsaved man, for I know perfectly well he will break it if he signs it. Usually when a man is thoroughly converted he hardly needs a pledge, though I believe the pledge is helpful in some cases. We do have meetings especially for drunkards. Usually we hold a meeting about midnight and sweep the streets and saloons, sending out workers and bands of music to gather them in. In one such meeting in Birmingham, England, there were about 3,000 drunkards present, most of them drunk at that time. Of these something like 180 professed to accept Christ at that meeting. The noisiest and most unmanageable one of all came forward and accepted Christ, and returned the next night so changed that hardly anyone knew him.

115

What shall a wife do whose husband continually drinks?

Go to God, and He will show her if there is anything in her that makes her husband drink. If she is cross and everything disagreeable in the home, while in the prayer meeting she seems everything sweet and angelic, she should first get thoroughly right with God herself, then get filled with the Holy Spirit, that she may show by the beauty of a Spirit-filled life the beauty of holiness. Her husband will be won and attracted to her by it. Then let her pray and watch her opportunity to speak to her husband, to move heaven and earth and never quit until he is converted.

THE THEATER

Is there any harm in a Christian going occasionally to see a good play?

There is a great difference between the different plays which are presented today. Some plays, and an increasingly large number of them, are utterly bad and demoralizing. Other plays are negative in their moral character, while still other plays are wholesome in their moral tone. So also there is a great difference between actors. Some actors and actresses are corrupt and corrupting, other actors and actresses are not nearly so bad, while it is to be hoped that there are actors and actresses who hold up before themselves high moral ideals and strive to live up to these ideals.

At first thought, then, it would seem as if there would be no harm in a Christian attending such plays as are morally uplifting in their tone and which are rendered by actors and actresses of unimpeachable character. But when one thinks more deeply on this question the problem is not so simple.

The theater as it exists today is an institution, and we must consider it as it actually is. It would be very easy to imagine a theater that would be positively helpful to the morals of a community, but the question is not what kind of a theater can we imagine but what kind of a theater exists today. The theater as it exists today is beyond a question an unclean